W9-AUY-922

Campbell's

100 top-rated RECIPES

pil
Publications
International, Ltd.

© **2012 Publications International, Ltd.**

Recipes and text © 2012 Campbell Soup Company.

Photographs on pages 9, 18, 31, 59, 61, 65, 67, 69, 81, 85, 87, 97, 105, 107, 109, 115, 130, 141, 155, 167, and 185 © 2012 Publications International, Ltd. and Campbell Soup Company. All other photography © Campbell Soup Company.

Campbell's®, Healthy Request®, Natural Goodness®, Pace®, Prego®, Swanson®, V8®, and *V8 V-Fusion®* registered trademarks of CSC Brands LP. All rights reserved.

Pepperidge Farm®, Bordeaux®, Chessman®, and *Milano®* registered trademarks of Pepperidge Farm, Incorporated. All rights reserved.

All rights reserved. This publication may not be reproduced or quoted in whole or in part by any means whatsoever without written permission from:

Louis Weber, CEO
Publications International, Ltd.
7373 North Cicero Avenue
Lincolnwood, IL 60712

Permission is never granted for commercial purposes.

Photography on pages 9, 18, 31, 59, 61, 65, 67, 69, 81, 85, 87, 97, 105, 107, 109, 115, 130, 141, 155, 167, and 185 by PIL Studio, Chicago.

Photographer: Annemarie Zelasko
Photographer's Assistant: Lauren Kessler
Prop Stylist: Paula Walters
Food Stylists: Mary Ann Melone, Carol Smoler
Assistant Food Stylists: Elaine Funk, Lissa Levy

Pictured on the front cover *(clockwise from center):* Green Bean Casserole *(page 152)*, Cheesy Chicken & Rice Casserole *(page 56)*, Slow Cooker Savory Pot Roast *(page 88)*, and Easy Chicken & Cheese Enchiladas *(page 60)*.

Pictured on the back cover *(clockwise from top):* Creamy Southwest Tomato Soup *(page 33)*, Berry Bordeaux Desserts *(page 187)*, Chicken with Picante Peach Sauce *(page 71)*, and Toasted Antipasto Sandwiches *(page 51)*.

ISBN-13: 978-1-4508-4645-5
ISBN-10: 1-4508-4645-9

Library of Congress Control Number: 2012930246

Manufactured in China.

8 7 6 5 4 3 2 1

Microwave Cooking: Microwave ovens vary in wattage. Use the cooking times as guidelines and check for doneness before adding more time.

Preparation/Cooking Times: Preparation times are based on the approximate amount of time required to assemble the recipe before cooking, baking, chilling or serving. These times include preparation steps such as measuring, chopping and mixing. The fact that some preparations and cooking can be done simultaneously is taken into account. Preparation of optional ingredients and serving suggestions is not included.

contents

100
top-rated recipes

What makes a recipe great?

You know those hand written recipe cards and dog-eared magazine pages that have become time-tested favorites—why do we come back to them again and again? Well, because the recipes taste terrific, of course, but other characteristics are important, too—they're easy to prepare and something the whole family will love. You just know that when a dish has those qualities, it's going to stand the test of time and become a regular part of your family's dinner rotation.

And that's why we're so excited to share this cookbook with you. In it are 100 of the highest-rated recipes from Campbell's Kitchen, recipes that cooks just like you—with busy families and busy schedules—enjoyed so much that they rated them with four or five stars so that other passionate cooks would want to try them too. These favorites encompass a wide range of tastes and preferences, from family-friendly to quick and easy to creative and different, and feature the entire family of Campbell's brands, which you've come to know and trust.

With a stamp of approval like that, you can be sure that this assortment of favorites will soon become as well-used as those in your personal recipe box! So let this cookbook inspire you—Campbell's can help you with whatever you need to see that your family is well-nourished and satisfied while making lasting memories around the dinner table.

Whatever the occasion, we've got appetizers

to match—from casual bites and dips to perfectly

portioned pastry creations.

appetizers

White Tomato Herb Pizza

MAKES 2 SERVINGS

THAW
40 MINUTES

PREP
15 MINUTES

BAKE
20 MINUTES

½ **of a 17.3-ounce package Pepperidge Farm® Puff Pastry Sheets (1 sheet), thawed**

2 **tablespoons olive oil**

¼ **cup grated Parmesan cheese**

⅔ **cup ricotta cheese**

2 **medium plum tomatoes, sliced**

2 **tablespoons chopped fresh basil leaves**

1 Heat the oven to 375°F. Line a baking sheet with parchment paper or spray with vegetable cooking spray.

2 Unfold the pastry on a lightly floured surface. Roll into a 9×13-inch rectangle. Cut the rectangle into **2** (4 ½×12-inch) rectangles. Roll in the edges to form a rim. Place the pastry rectangles on the baking sheet. Drizzle **each** with **1 tablespoon** olive oil.

3 Stir **2 tablespoons** Parmesan cheese and ricotta cheese in a small bowl.

4 Top **each** pastry rectangle with **half** the ricotta cheese mixture, **half** the tomatoes, **half** the basil and **half** the remaining Parmesan cheese.

5 Bake for 20 minutes or until the crust is golden.

Salsa Party Meatballs

MAKES 30 MEATBALLS

PREP
5 MINUTES

COOK
25 MINUTES

2½ **pounds ground beef *or* ground meat loaf mix (beef, pork *or* veal)**

6 **tablespoons dry bread crumbs**

¼ **cup milk**

2 **eggs**

1 **teaspoon garlic powder**

4 **green onions, chopped (about ½ cup)**

1 **cup shredded Cheddar cheese (about 4 ounces)**

2 **tablespoons olive *or* vegetable oil**

2 **jars (16 ounces *each*) Pace® Picante Sauce**

1 Mix the beef, bread crumbs, milk, eggs, garlic powder, green onions and **2 tablespoons** cheese thoroughly in a large bowl. Shape firmly into **30** (1½-inch) meatballs.

2 Heat the oil in a 12-inch nonstick skillet over medium-high heat. Add the meatballs and cook until they're well browned. Pour off any fat.

3 Stir the picante sauce in the skillet and heat to a boil. Reduce the heat to low. Cover and cook for 10 minutes or until the meatballs are cooked through. Stir in the remaining cheese and cook for 1 minute or until the cheese is melted. Sprinkle with additional chopped green onions, if desired. Serve with toothpicks.

Single-Serve Southwest Dip Cups

MAKES 24 SERVINGS

PREP
20 MINUTES

24 **foil baking cups (2½-inch)**

1 **can (about 16 ounces) refried beans**

2 **jars (11 ounces *each*) Pace® Chunky Salsa**

3 **medium avocados, peeled, pitted and chopped (about 1½ cups)**

1½ **cups shredded Cheddar cheese (about 6 ounces)**

1½ **cups sour cream**

½ **cup chopped fresh cilantro leaves**

Bite-sized tortilla chips

1 Place the foil cups onto a serving platter.

2 Layer **about 1 tablespoon each** beans, salsa, avocado and cheese into **each** cup. Top **each** with **about 1 tablespoon** sour cream and **about 1 teaspoon** cilantro. Serve with the tortilla chips for dipping.

Stop traffic jams around the dip bowl! Spoon a few tablespoons
of favorite dips into foil baking cups. Guests can cruise
by the serving table and pick up a dip cup and some dippers
and move on to mingle with other guests.

Savory Stuffed Mushrooms

MAKES 24 APPETIZERS

PREP
30 MINUTES

BAKE
10 MINUTES

24 **medium mushrooms**

6 **tablespoons butter** *or* **margarine**

1 **small onion, chopped (about** ¼ **cup)**

½ **teaspoon garlic powder** *or* **2 cloves garlic, minced**

1 **package (3 ounces) cream cheese, softened**

3 **tablespoons grated Parmesan cheese**

2 **tablespoons chopped fresh parsley** *or* **2 teaspoons dried parsley flakes**

1 **cup Pepperidge Farm® Herb Seasoned Stuffing**

tip

To make ahead, prepare as directed, but do not bake. Cover and refrigerate for up to 24 hours. Bake as directed.

1 Heat the oven to 425°F. Remove the stems from the mushrooms. Chop enough stems to make **1 cup**.

2 Heat **2 tablespoons** butter in a 2-quart saucepan over medium heat until it's melted. Brush the mushroom caps with the butter and place, top-side down, into a 3-quart shallow baking pan.

3 Heat the remaining butter in the saucepan until it's melted. Stir in the chopped mushroom stems, onion and garlic powder and cook until the mushrooms are tender. Stir in the cream cheese, Parmesan cheese and parsley. Add the stuffing and mix lightly. Spoon **about 1 tablespoon** stuffing mixture into **each** mushroom cap.

4 Bake for 10 minutes or until the filling is hot.

Buffalo Chicken Dip

MAKES 32 SERVINGS (4 CUPS)

PREP
10 MINUTES

BAKE
20 MINUTES

tips

This dip can be kept warm in a small slow cooker or fondue pot on the buffet table.

To reduce the fat use ⅓ less fat cream cheese and reduced-fat blue cheese salad dressing.

1 **package (8 ounces) cream cheese, softened**

½ **cup blue cheese salad dressing**

½ **cup hot pepper sauce**

2 **ounces crumbled blue cheese *or* shredded mozzarella cheese (about ½ cup)**

2 **cans (12.5 ounces *each*) Swanson® Premium White Chunk Chicken Breast in Water, drained**

Assorted fresh vegetables *and* Pepperidge Farm® crackers

1 Heat the oven to 350°F.

2 Stir the cream cheese in a 9-inch deep dish pie plate with a fork or whisk until it's smooth. Stir in the dressing, hot sauce and blue cheese. Stir in the chicken.

3 Bake for 20 minutes or until the chicken mixture is hot and bubbling. Stir the chicken mixture before serving. Serve with the vegetables and crackers for dipping.

To make in the microwave: Use a microwavable 9-inch deep dish pie plate. Prepare the dip as directed above in step 2. Microwave, uncovered, on HIGH for 5 minutes or until the chicken mixture is hot, stirring halfway through the cook time.

Sunset Dip

MAKES 12 SERVINGS (1½ CUPS)

1 **package (8 ounces) cream cheese, softened**

4 **ounces shredded Cheddar cheese (about 1 cup)**

1 **cup Pace® Picante Sauce *or* Pace® Chunky Salsa**

Tortilla chips

PREP
5 MINUTES

COOK
2 MINUTES

1 Spread the cream cheese in a 9-inch microwavable pie plate. Sprinkle with the Cheddar cheese.

2 Microwave on HIGH for 2 minutes or until the Cheddar cheese is melted. Top with the picante sauce. Serve with the tortilla chips.

Puff Pastry-Wrapped Brie

MAKES 6 SERVINGS

THAW
40 MINUTES

PREP
10 MINUTES

BAKE
25 MINUTES

STAND
20 MINUTES

½ **of a 17.3-ounce package Pepperidge Farm® Puff Pastry Sheets (1 sheet), thawed**

1 **(8-ounce) Brie cheese round**

1 **egg**

1 **tablespoon water**

1 Heat the oven to 400°F. Unfold the pastry sheet on a lightly floured surface. Place the cheese in the center. Fold the pastry up over the cheese to cover. Trim the excess pastry and press to seal. Reserve the pastry scraps for decoration.

2 Beat the egg and water in a small bowl with a fork or whisk. Brush the seam of the pastry with the egg mixture. Place seam-side down onto a baking sheet. Decorate with the pastry scraps, if desired. Brush with the egg mixture.

3 Bake for 25 minutes or until the pastry is golden brown. Let stand for 20 minutes.

Curried Chicken Spread

MAKES 10 SERVINGS (1¼ CUPS)

- 3 **tablespoons nonfat mayonnaise**
- 3 **tablespoons chopped chutney**
- ¼ **teaspoon curry powder**
- 1 **can (4.5 ounces) Swanson® Premium Chunk Chicken Breast in Water, drained**
- ½ **cup chopped Granny Smith apple**
- 1 **tablespoon chopped, unsalted dry roasted peanuts**

PREP
10 MINUTES

Stir the mayonnaise, chutney, curry powder, chicken, apple and peanuts in a small bowl.

Salsa Onion Dip

MAKES 24 SERVINGS (ABOUT 3 CUPS)

PREP
5 MINUTES

CHILL
2 HOURS

1 **envelope (about 1 ounce) dry onion soup and recipe mix**

1 **container (16 ounces) sour cream**

1 **cup Pace® Chunky Salsa**

Sliced green onion

Tortilla chips *or* fresh vegetables

Stir the soup mix, sour cream and salsa in a medium bowl. Cover and refrigerate for 2 hours. Sprinkle with the onion. Serve with the tortilla chips for dipping.

Spinach Onion Dip

MAKES 20 SERVINGS (ABOUT 2½ CUPS)

1 **envelope (about 1 ounce) dry onion soup and recipe mix**

1 **container (16 ounces) sour cream**

1 **package (about 10 ounces) frozen chopped spinach, thawed and well drained**

⅓ **cup chopped toasted almonds (optional)**

Assorted Pepperidge Farm® Crackers, chips *or* fresh vegetables

Stir the soup mix, sour cream, spinach and almonds, if desired, in a medium bowl. Cover and refrigerate for 2 hours. Serve with the crackers for dipping.

| PREP |
| 10 MINUTES |
| CHILL |
| 2 HOURS |

To thaw the spinach, microwave on HIGH for 3 minutes, breaking apart with a fork halfway through heating.

Whether you're in the mood for a hot, comforting

homemade soup or a hearty stew, we have plenty

you're sure to add to your favorites.

soups
& stews

Crab and Corn Chowder

MAKES 6 SERVINGS

PREP
15 MINUTES

COOK
35 MINUTES

4 slices bacon

1 large sweet onion, coarsely chopped (about 1 cup)

2 cloves garlic, minced

6 cups Swanson® Chicken Broth (Regular, Natural Goodness® *or* Certified Organic)

2 teaspoons seafood seasoning

6 to 8 red potatoes *or* fingerling potatoes, cut into 1-inch pieces (about 2 cups)

2 cups frozen whole kernel corn

1 container (8 ounces) refrigerated pasteurized lump crabmeat

½ cup heavy cream

*If you can't find sweet onions, regular white **or** yellow onions will work in this recipe.*

1 Cook the bacon in a 4-quart saucepan over medium-high heat for 5 minutes or until it's crisp. Remove the bacon with a fork or kitchen tongs and drain on paper towels. Crumble the bacon and set aside. Pour off all but **2 tablespoons** drippings.

2 Reduce the heat to medium. Add the onion and garlic to the saucepan and cook until the onion is tender.

3 Stir the broth, seafood seasoning, potatoes and corn in the saucepan. Heat to a boil. Reduce the heat to low and cook for 15 minutes or until the potatoes are tender.

4 Stir in the crabmeat and cream and cook for 5 minutes or until the mixture is hot and bubbling. Divide the chowder among **6** serving bowls. Top **each** with **about 1 tablespoon** bacon.

Hearty Chicken Tortilla Soup

MAKES 6 SERVINGS

PREP
10 MINUTES

COOK
30 MINUTES

Vegetable cooking spray

4 **skinless, boneless chicken breasts, cut into 1-inch pieces (about 1 pound)**

3½ **cups Swanson® Chicken Broth (Regular, Natural Goodness® or Certified Organic)**

1 **teaspoon ground cumin**

½ **cup uncooked regular long-grain white rice**

1 **can (11 ounces) whole kernel corn with red and green peppers, drained**

1 **cup Pace® Picante Sauce**

1 **tablespoon chopped fresh cilantro leaves**

2 **tablespoons fresh lime juice**

Crisp Tortilla Strips

Use a pastry wheel when cutting the tortillas to create a special touch for the soup garnish.

1 Spray a 6-quart saucepot with the cooking spray. Heat over medium-high heat for 1 minute. Add the chicken to the saucepot. Cook until it's browned, stirring often.

2 Stir the broth, cumin and rice in the saucepot. Heat to a boil. Reduce the heat to low. Cover and cook for 20 minutes.

3 Stir the corn, picante sauce, cilantro and lime juice in the saucepot. Cook until the rice is tender. Top **each** serving of soup with *Crisp Tortilla Strips.*

Crisp Tortilla Strips: Heat the oven to 425°F. Cut **4** corn tortillas into thin strips and place them on a baking sheet. Spray with the cooking spray. Bake for 10 minutes or until golden.

Spicy Peanut Soup

MAKES 8 SERVINGS

PREP
15 MINUTES

COOK
30 MINUTES

2 **tablespoons vegetable oil**

2 **large onions, diced (about 2 cups)**

2 **large carrots, diced (about 1 cup)**

1 **tablespoon minced fresh ginger root**

¼ **teaspoon ground red pepper**

6 **cups Swanson® Chicken Broth (Regular, Natural Goodness® *or* Certified Organic)**

2 **large sweet potatoes, peeled and diced (about 3 cups)**

1 **cup creamy peanut butter**

⅓ **cup sliced green onions *or* chives**

⅓ **cup chopped peanuts**

1 Heat the oil in a 4-quart saucepot over medium heat. Add the onions, carrots and ginger and cook until they're tender-crisp. Add the red pepper and cook for 1 minute.

2 Stir the broth and sweet potatoes in the saucepot. Heat to a boil. Reduce the heat to low. Cover and cook for 20 minutes or until the vegetables are tender. Stir in the peanut butter.

3 Place ⅓ of the broth mixture in a blender or food processor. Cover and blend until smooth. Pour into a large bowl. Repeat the blending process twice more with the remaining broth mixture. Return all of the puréed mixture to the saucepot. Cook over medium heat until the mixture is hot. Season to taste. Divide the soup among **8** serving bowls. Top **each** serving of soup with the green onions and peanuts.

Herb-Simmered Beef Stew

MAKES 6 SERVINGS

PREP
15 MINUTES
COOK
1 HOUR
30 MINUTES

2 **pounds beef for stew, cut into 1-inch cubes**

   Ground black pepper

2 **tablespoons all-purpose flour**

2 **tablespoons olive oil**

3 **cups thickly sliced mushrooms (about 8 ounces)**

3 **cloves garlic, minced**

½ **teaspoon dried marjoram leaves, crushed _or_**
   1½ teaspoons fresh marjoram leaves

½ **teaspoon dried thyme leaves, crushed _or_**
   1½ teaspoons fresh thyme leaves

½ **teaspoon dried rosemary leaves, crushed _or_**
   1½ teaspoons fresh rosemary leaves

1 **bay leaf**

1¾ **cups Swanson® Beef Stock**

3 **cups fresh _or_ frozen whole baby carrots**

12 **whole small red potatoes**

tip

For visual interest, you can peel a strip around the centers of the potatoes before cooking.

1 Season the beef with the black pepper. Coat the beef with the flour.

2 Heat the oil in a 6-quart saucepot over medium-high heat. Add the beef in 2 batches and cook until it's well browned, stirring often. Pour off any fat.

3 Add the mushrooms, garlic, herbs and bay leaf to the saucepot and cook until the mushrooms are tender. Stir in the stock and heat to a boil. Reduce the heat to low. Cover and cook for 45 minutes.

4 Increase the heat to medium-high. Stir in the carrots and potatoes and heat to a boil. Reduce the heat to low. Cover and cook for 30 minutes or until the beef is fork-tender. Remove and discard the bay leaf.

Chilled Picante Gazpacho

MAKES 4 SERVINGS

PREP
15 MINUTES

CHILL
2 HOURS

1 **can (28 ounces) whole peeled tomatoes**

¾ **cup Pace® Picante Sauce**

2 **tablespoons lemon juice**

1 **tablespoon chopped fresh cilantro leaves**

¼ **teaspoon garlic powder *or* 1 clove garlic, minced**

1 **cup thickly sliced cucumber**

1 **stalk celery, cut into 1-inch pieces**

1 **slice firm Pepperidge Farm® White Sandwich Bread**

¼ **cup chopped cucumber**

Sliced green onions

1 Place the tomatoes, picante sauce, lemon juice, cilantro, garlic powder, sliced cucumber, celery and bread into a blender or food processor. Cover and blend until smooth. Refrigerate for at least 2 hours.

2 Top with the chopped cucumber. Garnish with the onions.

Creamy Southwest Tomato Soup

MAKES 6 SERVINGS

2 **cans (10¾ ounces *each*) Campbell's® Condensed Tomato Soup**

2 **soup cans milk**

1 **jar (16 ounces) Pace® Picante Sauce**

PREP
5 MINUTES

COOK
5 MINUTES

Heat the soup, milk and picante sauce in a 3-quart saucepan over medium heat until the mixture is hot and bubbling.

Bacon Potato Chowder

MAKES 8 SERVINGS

PREP
15 MINUTES

COOK
3 HOURS

4 slices bacon, cooked and crumbled

1 large onion, chopped (about 1 cup)

4 cans (10¾ ounces *each*) Campbell's® Condensed Cream of Potato Soup

4 soup cans milk

¼ teaspoon ground black pepper

2 large russet potatoes, cut into ½-inch pieces (about 3 cups)

½ cup chopped fresh chives

2 cups shredded Cheddar cheese (about 8 ounces)

1 Stir the bacon, onion, soup, milk, black pepper, potatoes and ¼ **cup** chives in a 6-quart slow cooker.

2 Cover and cook on HIGH for 3 to 4 hours or until the potatoes are tender.

3 Add the cheese and stir until the cheese is melted. Serve with the remaining chives.

Cheeseburger Chowder

MAKES 8 SERVINGS

1 **pound ground beef**

1 **large onion, chopped (about 1 cup)**

2 **cans (26 ounces *each*) Campbell's® Condensed Cream
   of Mushroom Soup (Regular *or* 98% Fat Free)**

2 **soup cans milk**

1 **cup finely shredded Cheddar cheese**

1 **cup Pepperidge Farm® Seasoned Croutons**

PREP
10 MINUTES

COOK
20 MINUTES

1 Cook the beef and onion in a 3-quart saucepan over
medium-high heat until the beef is well browned, stirring
often to separate the meat. Pour off any fat.

2 Stir the soup and milk in the saucepan. Cook until the
mixture is hot and bubbling. Stir in ½ **cup** cheese. Cook and
stir until the cheese is melted.

3 Divide the soup among **8** serving bowls. Top each bowl
with **1 tablespoon** remaining cheese and **2 tablespoons**
croutons.

French Onion Soup

MAKES 4 SERVINGS

PREP
10 MINUTES

COOK
45 MINUTES

1 **tablespoon vegetable oil**

2½ **large onions, halved and thinly sliced (about 2½ cups)***

¼ **teaspoon sugar**

2 **tablespoons all-purpose flour**

3½ **cups Swanson® Beef Broth (Regular, Lower Sodium or Certified Organic)**

¼ **cup dry white wine or vermouth**

4 **slices French bread, toasted****

½ **cup shredded Swiss cheese**

Use a food processor with slicing attachment for ease in preparation.
**For even more flavor, try rubbing the bread with a garlic clove and topping it with the cheese before toasting.*

1 Heat the oil in a 4-quart saucepot over medium heat. Add the onions. Reduce the heat to low. Cover and cook for 15 minutes. Uncover the saucepot.

2 Increase the heat to medium. Add the sugar and cook for 15 minutes or until the onions are golden.

3 Stir the flour in the saucepot and cook and stir for 1 minute. Stir in the broth and wine. Heat to a boil. Reduce the heat to low. Cook for 10 minutes.

4 Divide the soup among 4 bowls. Top **each** with a bread slice and cheese.

Sensational Chicken Noodle Soup

MAKES 4 SERVINGS

PREP
5 MINUTES

COOK
25 MINUTES

4 cups Swanson® Chicken Broth (Regular, Natural Goodness® *or* Certified Organic)

Generous dash ground black pepper

1 **medium carrot, sliced (about ½ cup)**

1 **stalk celery, sliced (about ½ cup)**

½ **cup *uncooked* extra-wide egg noodles**

1 **cup shredded cooked chicken *or* turkey**

1 Heat the broth, black pepper, carrot and celery in a 2-quart saucepan over medium-high heat to a boil.

2 Stir the noodles and chicken into the saucepan. Reduce the heat to medium. Cook for 10 minutes or until the noodles are tender.

Asian Soup: Add **2** green onions cut into ½-inch pieces, **1** clove garlic, minced, **1 teaspoon** ground ginger and **2 teaspoons** soy sauce. Substitute **uncooked** curly Asian noodles for egg noodles.

Mexican Soup: Add ½ **cup** Pace® Chunky Salsa, **1** clove garlic, minced, **1 cup** rinsed and drained black beans and ½ **teaspoon** chili powder. Substitute **2** corn tortillas (4 or 6-inch) cut into thin strips for the noodles, adding them just before serving.

Italian Tortellini Soup: Add **1 can** (about 14.5 ounces) diced tomatoes, drained, **1** clove garlic, minced, **1 teaspoon** dried Italian seasoning, crushed, and **1 cup** spinach leaves. Substitute ½ **cup** frozen cheese tortellini for egg noodles. Serve with grated Parmesan cheese.

Easy to make and endless in variety,

sandwiches are the perfect lunchtime pick.

sandwiches

Turkey Fajita Wraps

MAKES 8 SERVINGS

<table>
<tr><td rowspan="4">

PREP
10 MINUTES

COOK
6 HOURS

</td></tr>
</table>

2	**cups Pace® Picante Sauce**
2	**large green *or* red peppers, cut into 2-inch-long strips (about 4 cups)**
1½	**cups frozen whole kernel corn, thawed**
1	**tablespoon chili powder**
2	**tablespoons lime juice**
3	**cloves garlic, minced**
2	**pounds turkey breast cutlets, cut into 4-inch-long strips**
16	**flour tortillas (8-inch), warmed**
	Shredded Mexican cheese blend

1 Stir the picante sauce, peppers, corn, chili powder, lime juice, garlic and turkey in a 4-quart slow cooker.

2 Cover and cook on LOW for 6 to 7 hours* or until the turkey is cooked through.

3 Spoon **about ½ cup** of the turkey mixture down the center of **each** tortilla. Top with the cheese. Fold the tortillas around the filling.

Or on HIGH for 3 to 4 hours.

---

*Delicious served with an assortment of additional toppers: sliced green onions, sliced ripe olives, shredded lettuce, sliced jalapeño peppers, sour cream **and/or** chopped fresh cilantro.*

Italian Sausage Sandwiches

MAKES 4 SERVINGS

PREP
5 MINUTES

COOK
15 MINUTES

1 **pound Italian pork sausage, casing removed**

1½ **cups Prego® Chunky Garden Mushroom & Green Pepper Italian Sauce**

4 **long hard rolls, split**

1 Cook the sausage in a 10-inch skillet over medium-high heat until it's well browned, stirring often to separate the meat. Pour off any fat.

2 Stir in the Italian sauce and cook until the mixture is hot and bubbling. Serve the sausage mixture on the rolls.

You can use any favorite Prego® Italian Sauce in this recipe.

Breakfast Omelet Sandwiches

MAKES 2 SERVINGS

PREP
25 MINUTES

COOK
20 MINUTES

Vegetable cooking spray

½ **cup chopped fresh mushrooms**

¼ **cup chopped green pepper**

¼ **cup chopped tomato**

2 **tablespoons finely chopped onions**

½ **cup cholesterol-free egg substitute**

2 **teaspoons freshly grated Parmesan cheese**

4 **slices Pepperidge Farm® 100% Natural Nine Grain Bread**

Also delicious with Pepperidge Farm® Whole Grain 15 Grain Bread.

1 Spray an 8-inch nonstick skillet with the cooking spray and heat over medium heat for 1 minute. Add the mushrooms, pepper, tomato and onion. Cover and cook until the vegetables are tender. Remove the vegetables from the skillet. Remove the skillet from the heat. Wipe out the skillet with a paper towel.

2 Spray the skillet with the cooking spray and heat over medium heat for 1 minute. Add ¼ **cup** egg substitute and top with **half** the cooked vegetables. Cook until the eggs are set but still moist on top, lifting the edges of the omelet with a spatula. Sprinkle with **half** of the cheese. Fold the omelet in half. Place the omelet on **1** bread slice and top with another bread slice. Repeat with the remaining ingredients.

Spring Garden Vegetable Sandwiches

MAKES 2 SERVINGS

4 **tablespoons Neufchâtel cheese, softened**

4 **slices Pepperidge Farm® 100% Natural Honey Flax Bread, toasted**

1 **medium cucumber, peeled and thinly sliced (about 1²/₃ cups)**

2 **medium carrots, shredded (about 1 cup)**

1 **cup spring salad mix**

1 **green onion, thinly sliced (about 2 tablespoons)**

3 **tablespoons fat-free sun-dried tomato salad dressing**

PREP
15 MINUTES

1 Spread the cheese on the bread slices.

2 Arrange the cucumber on **2** bread slices. Place the carrots, spring mix and onions in a medium bowl. Add the dressing and toss to coat. Top the cucumber with the carrot mixture and the remaining bread slices.

Bagel Bruschetta

MAKES 1 SERVING

PREP
10 MINUTES

COOK
2 MINUTES

2 **teaspoons olive oil**

1 **bagel Pepperidge Farm® 100% Whole Wheat Bagels, split**

1 **clove garlic, cut in half**

1 **tomato, diced**

1 **tablespoon chopped fresh basil leaves**

   Freshly ground black pepper

1 Brush the oil on the cut sides of the bagel halves.

2 Heat the broiler. Broil, cut-side up, for 2 minutes or until the bagel halves are toasted. Rub the garlic on the cut sides of the bagel halves.

3 Stir the tomato and basil in a small bowl. Season with the black pepper. Divide the tomato mixture between the bagel halves.

Quick Chicken Mozzarella Sandwiches

MAKES 4 SERVINGS

1½ **cups Prego® Three Cheese Italian Sauce**

4 **refrigerated _or_ thawed frozen cooked breaded chicken cutlets**

4 **slices mozzarella cheese**

4 **round hard rolls**

PREP
5 MINUTES

COOK
15 MINUTES

1 Heat the Italian sauce in a 10-inch skillet over medium heat to a boil. Place the chicken in the sauce. Reduce the heat to low. Cover and cook for 5 minutes or until the chicken is heated through.

2 Top the chicken with the cheese. Cover and cook until the cheese is melted. Serve on the rolls.

Spinach and Feta Mini-Calzones

MAKES 16 SERVINGS

THAW
40 MINUTES

PREP
30 MINUTES

BAKE
15 MINUTES

COOL
10 MINUTES

½ **of a 17.3-ounce package Pepperidge Farm® Puff Pastry Sheets (1 sheet), thawed**

1 **tablespoon olive oil**

1 **small onion, chopped (about ¼ cup)**

1 **package (10 ounces) frozen chopped spinach, thawed and well drained**

½ **cup crumbled feta cheese (plain or flavored)**

¼ **teaspoon ground black pepper**

1 Heat the oven to 400°F.

2 Heat the oil in a 10-inch skillet over medium heat. Add the onion and cook until tender. Add the spinach and cook for 3 minutes. Remove the skillet from the heat. Stir in the cheese and black pepper. Let the mixture cool to room temperature.

3 Unfold the pastry sheet on a lightly floured surface. Roll the pastry sheet into a 12-inch square. Cut into **16** (3-inch) squares. Brush edges of the squares with water. Place **about 1 tablespoon** spinach mixture in the center of each square. Fold the pastry over the filling to form triangles. Press the edges to seal. Place the filled pastries onto a baking sheet.

4 Bake for 15 minutes or until the pastries are golden brown. Remove the pastries from the baking sheet and let cool on wire racks for 10 minutes.

Miami Chicken Salad Sandwiches

MAKES 2 SERVINGS

2 **tablespoons light mayonnaise**

2 **tablespoons reduced-fat sour cream**

1 **teaspoon dried tarragon leaves, crushed**

1 **can (4.5 ounces) Swanson® Premium White Chunk Chicken Breast in Water, drained**

¼ **cup slivered almonds, toasted**

¼ **cup chopped jicama *or* celery**

4 **slices Pepperidge Farm® Whole Grain Soft Honey Oat Bread, toasted***

1 **mango, pitted, peeled and sliced**

Green leaf lettuce leaves

Also delicious with Pepperidge Farm® 100% Natural Honey Flax Bread.

PREP
15 MINUTES

1 Stir the mayonnaise, sour cream and tarragon in a medium bowl. Stir in the chicken, almonds and jicama.

2 Divide the chicken mixture between **2** bread slices. Top with the mango, lettuce and remaining bread slices.

Mozzarella Meatball Sandwiches

MAKES 4 SERVINGS

PREP
15 MINUTES

BAKE
10 MINUTES

COOK
20 MINUTES

1 **loaf (11.75 ounces) Pepperidge Farm® Frozen Mozzarella Garlic Cheese Bread**

½ **cup Prego® Traditional Italian Sauce *or* Organic Tomato & Basil Italian Sauce**

12 **(½ ounce *each*) *or* 6 (1 ounce *each*) frozen meatballs**

1 Heat the oven to 400°F. Remove the bread from the bag. Carefully separate the bread halves with a fork. Place the 2 bread halves, cut-side up, onto a baking sheet.

2 Bake for 10 minutes or until the bread is heated through.

3 Heat the Italian sauce and meatballs in a 2-quart saucepan over low heat. Cook and stir for 20 minutes or until the meatballs are heated through. Spoon the meatball mixture onto the bottom bread half. Top with the top bread half. Cut into quarters.

Toasted Antipasto Sandwiches

MAKES 2 SERVINGS

2 **tablespoons prepared lowfat Italian salad dressing**

4 **slices Pepperidge Farm® Whole Grain 15 Grain Bread**

2 **ounces sliced deli reduced-sodium ham**

2 **ounces sliced part-skim mozzarella cheese**

¼ **cup drained jarred roasted red pepper strips**

1 **medium zucchini, thinly sliced (about 1½ cups)**

4 **fresh basil leaves, cut into thin strips**

Vegetable cooking spray

PREP
15 MINUTES

COOK
5 MINUTES

1 Spread the dressing on **2** bread slices. Top with the ham, cheese, peppers, zucchini, basil and remaining bread slices.

2 Spray a 10-inch nonstick skillet with the cooking spray and heat over medium heat for 1 minute. Add the sandwiches and cook until lightly browned on both sides and the cheese is melted.

Also delicious with Pepperidge Farm® 100% Natural Nine Grain Bread.

Easy-to-prepare, family-favorite

dinners are at your fingertips

when you start with chicken.

chicken

Chicken in Creamy Sun-Dried Tomato Sauce

MAKES 8 SERVINGS

PREP
15 MINUTES

COOK
7 HOURS

2 cans (10¾ ounces **each**) Campbell's® Condensed Cream of Chicken with Herbs Soup **or** Campbell's® Condensed Cream of Chicken Soup

1 cup Chablis **or** other dry white wine*

¼ cup coarsely chopped pitted kalamata **or** oil-cured olives

2 tablespoons drained capers

2 cloves garlic, minced

1 can (14 ounces) artichoke hearts, drained and chopped

1 cup drained and coarsely chopped sun-dried tomatoes

8 skinless, boneless chicken breast halves (about 2 pounds)

½ cup chopped fresh basil leaves (optional)

Hot cooked rice, egg noodles **or** mashed potatoes

You can substitute Swanson® Chicken Broth for the wine, if desired.

1 Stir the soup, wine, olives, capers, garlic, artichokes and tomatoes in a 3½-quart slow cooker. Add the chicken and turn to coat.

2 Cover and cook on LOW for 7 to 8 hours** or until the chicken is cooked through. Sprinkle with the basil, if desired. Serve with the rice.

**Or on HIGH for 4 to 5 hours.*

Cheesy Chicken & Rice Casserole

MAKES 4 SERVINGS

PREP
15 MINUTES

BAKE
50 MINUTES

STAND
10 MINUTES

1 **can (10¾ ounces) Campbell's® Condensed Cream of Chicken Soup (Regular, 98% Fat Free _or_ Healthy Request®)**

1⅓ **cups water**

¾ **cup _uncooked_ regular long-grain white rice**

½ **teaspoon onion powder**

¼ **teaspoon ground black pepper**

2 **cups frozen mixed vegetables**

4 **skinless, boneless chicken breast halves (about 1 pound)**

½ **cup shredded Cheddar cheese**

1 Heat the oven to 375°F. Stir the soup, water, rice, onion powder, black pepper and vegetables in a 2-quart shallow baking dish.

2 Top with the chicken. Cover the baking dish.

3 Bake for 50 minutes or until the chicken is cooked through and the rice is tender. Top with the cheese. Let the casserole stand for 10 minutes. Stir the rice before serving.

To Make Alfredo: Substitute broccoli florets for the vegetables and substitute ¼ **cup** grated Parmesan for the Cheddar cheese. Add **2 tablespoons** Parmesan cheese with the soup. Sprinkle the chicken with the remaining Parmesan cheese.

Lower Fat: Use Campbell's® 98% Fat Free Cream of Chicken Soup instead of regular soup and use low-fat cheese instead of regular cheese.

Mexican: In place of the onion powder and black pepper use **1 teaspoon** chili powder. Substitute Mexican cheese blend for the Cheddar.

Italian: In place of the onion powder and black pepper use **1 teaspoon** Italian seasoning, crushed. Substitute ⅓ **cup** shredded Parmesan for the Cheddar.

Chicken & Roasted Garlic Risotto

MAKES 4 SERVINGS

PREP
5 MINUTES

COOK
20 MINUTES

STAND
5 MINUTES

1 **tablespoon butter**

4 **skinless, boneless chicken breast halves (about 1 pound)**

1 **can (10¾ ounces) Campbell's® Condensed Cream of Chicken Soup (Regular *or* 98% Fat Free)**

1 **can (10¾ ounces) Campbell's® Condensed Cream of Mushroom with Roasted Garlic Soup**

2 **cups water**

2 **cups *uncooked* instant white rice**

1 **cup frozen peas and carrots**

1 Heat the butter in a 10-inch skillet over medium-high heat. Add the chicken and cook for 10 minutes or until it's well browned on both sides. Remove the chicken from the skillet.

2 Stir the soups and water in the skillet and heat to a boil. Stir in the rice and vegetables. Return the chicken to the skillet. Reduce the heat to low. Cover and cook for 5 minutes or until the chicken is cooked through. Remove the skillet from the heat. Let stand for 5 minutes.

Traditionally, risotto is made by sautéing rice in butter then stirring broth into the rice a little at a time—very labor-intensive. This dish gives you the same creamy texture with a lot less work!

Easy Chicken & Cheese Enchiladas

MAKES 6 SERVINGS

PREP
15 MINUTES

BAKE
40 MINUTES

1   **can (10¾ ounces) Campbell's® Condensed Cream of Chicken Soup (Regular *or* 98% Fat Free)**

½ **cup sour cream**

1   **cup Pace® Picante Sauce**

2   **teaspoons chili powder**

2   **cups chopped cooked chicken**

½ **cup shredded Monterey Jack cheese**

6   **flour tortillas (6-inch), warmed**

1   **small tomato, chopped (about ½ cup)**

1   **green onion, sliced (about 2 tablespoons)**

*Stir ½ **cup** canned black beans, rinsed and drained, into the chicken mixture before filling the tortillas.*

1 Heat the oven to 350°F. Stir the soup, sour cream, picante sauce and chili powder in a medium bowl.

2 Stir **1 cup** soup mixture, chicken and cheese in a large bowl.

3 Divide the chicken mixture among the tortillas. Roll up the tortillas and place, seam-side up, in a 2-quart shallow baking dish. Pour the remaining soup mixture over the filled tortillas. Cover the baking dish.

4 Bake for 40 minutes or until the enchiladas are hot and bubbling. Top with the tomato and onion.

Chicken & Broccoli Alfredo

MAKES 4 SERVINGS

PREP
10 MINUTES

COOK
20 MINUTES

$\frac{1}{2}$ **of a 16-ounce package linguine**

1 **cup fresh *or* frozen broccoli florets**

2 **tablespoons butter**

4 **skinless, boneless chicken breast halves (about 1 pound), cut into 1$\frac{1}{2}$-inch pieces**

1 **can (10$\frac{3}{4}$ ounces) Campbell's® Condensed Cream of Mushroom Soup (Regular, 98% Fat Free *or* Healthy Request®)**

$\frac{1}{2}$ **cup milk**

$\frac{1}{2}$ **cup grated Parmesan cheese**

$\frac{1}{4}$ **teaspoon ground black pepper**

*You can substitute spaghetti **or** fettuccine for the linguine in this recipe.*

1 Prepare the linguine according to the package directions in a 3-quart saucepan. Add the broccoli during the last 4 minutes of the cooking time. Drain the linguine mixture well in a colander.

2 Heat the butter in a 10-inch skillet over medium-high heat. Add the chicken and cook until it's well browned, stirring often.

3 Stir the soup, milk, cheese, black pepper and linguine mixture in the skillet and cook until the chicken is cooked through, stirring occasionally. Serve with additional Parmesan cheese.

Grilled Chicken & Broccoli Alfredo: Substitute grilled chicken breasts for the skinless, boneless chicken.

Shrimp & Broccoli Alfredo: Substitute **1 pound** fresh extra large shrimp, shelled and deveined, for the chicken. Cook as directed for the chicken above, until the shrimp are cooked through.

Spanish-Inspired: Reduce the chicken to $\frac{1}{2}$ **pound** and omit the Parmesan cheese. Prepare as directed above. Stir $\frac{1}{2}$ **pound** peeled cooked shrimp, $\frac{1}{4}$ **pound** chorizo or ham, diced, and **1 teaspoon** paprika into the soup mixture.

25-Minute Chicken & Noodles

MAKES 4 SERVINGS

PREP
5 MINUTES

COOK
20 MINUTES

1³/₄ **cups Swanson® Chicken Stock**

1 **teaspoon dried basil leaves, crushed**

¹/₄ **teaspoon ground black pepper**

2 **cups frozen vegetable combination (broccoli, cauliflower, carrots)**

2 **cups *uncooked* medium egg noodles**

2 **cups cubed cooked chicken**

1 Heat the stock, basil, black pepper and vegetables in a 10-inch skillet over medium heat to a boil. Reduce the heat to low. Cover and cook for 5 minutes or until the vegetables are tender-crisp.

2 Stir the noodles in the skillet. Cover and cook for 5 minutes or until the noodles are tender. Stir in the chicken and cook until the mixture is hot and bubbling.

Skillet Chicken Parmesan

MAKES 6 SERVINGS

PREP
5 MINUTES

COOK
20 MINUTES

STAND
5 MINUTES

¼ cup grated **Parmesan cheese**

1½ cups **Prego® Traditional *or* Organic Tomato & Basil Italian Sauce**

1 tablespoon **olive oil**

1½ pounds **skinless, boneless chicken breast halves**

1½ cups **shredded part-skim mozzarella cheese (about 6 ounces)**

1 Stir **3 tablespoons** of the Parmesan cheese and Italian sauce in a small bowl.

2 Heat the oil in a 12-inch skillet over medium-high heat. Add the chicken and cook for 10 minutes or until it's well browned on both sides.

3 Pour the sauce mixture over the chicken, turning to coat with the sauce. Reduce the heat to low. Cover and cook for 10 minutes or until chicken is cooked through.

4 Top with the mozzarella cheese and the remaining Parmesan cheese. Let stand for 5 minutes or until the cheese is melted.

Sweet & Spicy Picante Chicken

MAKES 4 SERVINGS

PREP
15 MINUTES

BAKE
20 MINUTES

 4 **skinless, boneless chicken breast halves (about 1 pound)**

1½ **cups Pace® Picante Sauce**

 3 **tablespoons packed light brown sugar**

 1 **tablespoon Dijon-style mustard**

 3 **cups hot cooked regular long-grain white rice**

1 Heat the oven to 400°F. Place the chicken into a 2-quart shallow baking dish. Stir the picante sauce, brown sugar and mustard in a small bowl. Pour the picante sauce mixture over the chicken.

2 Bake for 20 minutes or until the chicken is cooked through. Serve with the rice.

Maple Dijon Chicken

MAKES 4 SERVINGS

PREP
10 MINUTES

COOK
25 MINUTES

1 **tablespoon olive oil**

4 **skinless, boneless chicken breast halves (about 1 pound)**

2 **shallots, chopped (about ½ cup)**

2 **cloves garlic, minced**

1 **cup Swanson® Chicken Stock**

⅓ **cup maple-flavored syrup**

1 **tablespoon Dijon-style mustard**

⅛ **teaspoon crushed red pepper**

1 Heat the oil in a 12-inch skillet over medium-high heat. Add the chicken and cook for 15 minutes or until it's well browned on both sides and cooked through. Remove the chicken from the skillet.

2 Add the shallots and garlic to the skillet and cook until they're tender. Stir in the stock, syrup, mustard and pepper and heat to a boil. Reduce the heat to low. Cook for 10 minutes or until the stock mixture is slightly thickened and reduced to **about 1 cup**. Serve the stock mixture over the chicken.

Chicken with Picante Peach Salsa

MAKES 6 SERVINGS

⅓ cup Pace® Picante Sauce

2 tablespoons lime juice

1 can (about 15 ounces) peach halves in heavy syrup, drained and diced

⅓ cup chopped green *or* red pepper

2 green onions, sliced (about ¼ cup)

½ teaspoon ground cumin

½ teaspoon chili powder

6 skinless, boneless chicken breast halves

½ cup peach preserves *or* apricot preserves

PREP
10 MINUTES

GRILL
15 MINUTES

1 Stir ⅓ **cup** picante sauce, lime juice, peaches, pepper and onions in a medium bowl. Reserve the mixture to serve with the chicken.

2 Stir the cumin and chili powder in a small bowl. Season the chicken with the cumin mixture. Stir the remaining picante sauce and preserves in a small bowl.

3 Lightly oil the grill rack and heat the grill to medium. Grill the chicken for 15 minutes or until it's cooked through, turning and brushing often with the preserve mixture. Discard the remaining preserve mixture.

4 Serve the chicken with the peach salsa mixture.

Nothing compares with the juicy, delicious

flavor of beef—it's always a hit at dinner.

beef

Chipotle Chili

MAKES 8 SERVINGS

PREP
15 MINUTES

COOK
8 HOURS

1 **jar (16 ounces) Pace® Picante Sauce**

1 **cup water**

2 **tablespoons chili powder**

1 **teaspoon ground chipotle chile pepper**

1 **large onion, chopped (about 1 cup)**

2 **pounds beef for stew, cut into $\frac{1}{2}$-inch pieces**

1 **can (about 19 ounces) red kidney beans, rinsed and drained**

Shredded Cheddar cheese (optional)

Sour cream (optional)

1 Stir the picante sauce, water, chili powder, chipotle pepper, onion, beef and beans in a $3\frac{1}{2}$-quart slow cooker.

2 Cover and cook on LOW for 8 to 9 hours* or until the beef is fork-tender. Serve with the cheese and sour cream, if desired.

Or on HIGH for 4 to 5 hours.

Beef Bourguignonne

MAKES 6 SERVINGS

PREP
10 MINUTES

COOK
8 HOURS

1 **can (10¾ ounces) Campbell's® Condensed Golden Mushroom Soup**

1 **cup Burgundy *or* other dry red wine**

2 **cloves garlic, minced**

1 **teaspoon dried thyme leaves, crushed**

2 **cups small button mushrooms (about 6 ounces)**

2 **cups fresh *or* thawed frozen baby carrots**

1 **cup frozen small whole onions, thawed**

1½ **pounds beef top round steak, 1½-inches thick, cut into 1-inch pieces**

1 Stir the soup, wine, garlic, thyme, mushrooms, carrots, onions and beef in a 3½-quart slow cooker.

2 Cover and cook on LOW for 8 to 9 hours* or until the beef is fork-tender.

Or on HIGH for 4 to 5 hours.

Melt-in-Your-Mouth Short Ribs

MAKES 6 SERVINGS

PREP
10 MINUTES

COOK
8 HOURS

6 **serving-sized pieces beef short ribs (about 3 pounds)**

2 **tablespoons packed brown sugar**

3 **cloves garlic, minced**

1 **teaspoon dried thyme leaves, crushed**

¼ **cup all-purpose flour**

1 **can (10½ ounces) Campbell's® Condensed French Onion Soup**

1 **bottle (12 fluid ounces) dark ale *or* beer**

   Hot mashed potatoes *or* egg noodles

1 Place the beef into a 5-quart slow cooker. Add the brown sugar, garlic, thyme and flour and toss to coat.

2 Stir the soup and ale in a small bowl. Pour over the beef.

3 Cover and cook on LOW for 8 to 9 hours* or until the beef is fork-tender. Serve with the mashed potatoes.

Or on HIGH for 4 to 5 hours.

Cheeseburger Pasta

MAKES 5 SERVINGS

PREP
5 MINUTES

COOK
20 MINUTES

1 **pound ground beef**

1 **can (10¾ ounces) Campbell's® Condensed Cheddar Cheese Soup**

1 **can (10¾ ounces) Campbell's® Condensed Tomato Soup (Regular *or* Healthy Request®)**

1½ **cups water**

2 **cups *uncooked* medium shell-shaped pasta**

1 Cook the beef in a 10-inch skillet over medium-high heat until well browned, stirring often to separate the meat. Pour off any fat.

2 Stir the soups, water and pasta in the skillet and heat to a boil. Reduce the heat to medium. Cook for 10 minutes or until the pasta is tender, stirring often.

Beef Stroganoff

MAKES 4 SERVINGS

PREP
10 MINUTES

COOK
25 MINUTES

1 **tablespoon vegetable oil**

1 **boneless beef sirloin steak *or* beef top round steak, ³/₄-inch thick (about 1 pound), cut into thin strips**

1 **medium onion, chopped (about ½ cup)**

1 **can (10³/₄ ounces) Campbell's® Condensed Cream of Mushroom Soup (Regular, 98% Fat Free *or* Healthy Request®)**

½ **teaspoon paprika**

⅓ **cup sour cream *or* plain yogurt**

4 **cups whole wheat *or* regular egg noodles, cooked and drained**

Chopped fresh parsley

1 Heat the oil in a 12-inch nonstick skillet over medium-high heat. Add the beef and cook until well browned, stirring often. Remove the beef from the skillet. Pour off any fat.

2 Reduce the heat to medium. Add the onion to the skillet and cook until it's tender.

3 Stir the soup and paprika in the skillet and heat to a boil. Stir in the sour cream. Return the beef to the skillet and cook until the beef is cooked through. Serve the beef mixture over the noodles. Sprinkle with the parsley.

Best Ever Meatloaf

MAKES 8 SERVINGS

PREP
10 MINUTES

BAKE
1 HOUR
15 MINUTES

COOK
5 MINUTES

STAND
10 MINUTES

2 pounds ground beef

1 can (10¾ ounces) Campbell's® Condensed Tomato Soup (Regular *or* Healthy Request®)

1 envelope (about 1 ounce) dry onion soup and recipe mix

½ cup dry bread crumbs

1 egg, beaten

¼ cup water

1 Thoroughly mix the beef, ½ **cup** tomato soup, onion soup mix, bread crumbs and egg in a large bowl. Place the mixture into a 13×9×2-inch baking pan and firmly shape into an 8×4-inch loaf.

2 Bake at 350°F. for 1 hour 15 minutes or until the meatloaf is cooked through. Let the meatloaf stand for 10 minutes before slicing.

3 Heat **2 tablespoons** pan drippings, remaining tomato soup and water in a 1-quart saucepan over medium heat until the mixture is hot and bubbling. Serve the sauce with the meatloaf.

*You can substitute Campbell's® Condensed Cream of Mushroom Soup (Regular **or** 98% Fat Free) for the Tomato Soup.*

Shortcut Beef Stew

MAKES 4 SERVINGS

PREP
5 MINUTES

COOK
25 MINUTES

1 **tablespoon vegetable oil**

1 **boneless beef sirloin steak, ³/₄-inch thick (about 1 pound), cut into 1-inch pieces**

1 **can (10³/₄ ounces) Campbell's® Condensed Tomato Soup**

1 **can (10¹/₂ ounces) Campbell's® Condensed French Onion Soup**

1 **tablespoon Worcestershire sauce**

1 **bag (24 ounces) frozen vegetables for stew (potatoes, carrots, celery, peas)**

1 Heat the oil in a 10-inch skillet over medium-high heat. Add the beef and cook until well browned, stirring often. Pour off any fat.

2 Stir the soups, Worcestershire and vegetables in the skillet and heat to a boil. Reduce the heat to low. Cover and cook for 10 minutes or until the beef is cooked through and the vegetables are tender.

tips

*Substitute **5 cups** frozen vegetables (carrots, small whole onions, cut green beans, cauliflower, zucchini, peas **or** lima beans) for the frozen vegetables in stew.*

Substitute Campbell's® Condensed Beefy Mushroom Soup for the French Onion Soup.

Slow Cooker Savory Pot Roast

MAKES 6 SERVINGS

PREP
10 MINUTES

COOK
8 HOURS

1   can (10¾ ounces) Campbell's® Condensed Cream of Mushroom Soup (Regular *or* 98% Fat Free)

1   envelope (about 1 ounce) dry onion soup and recipe mix

6   small red potatoes, cut in half

6   medium carrots, cut into 2-inch pieces (about 3 cups)

1   boneless beef bottom round roast *or* chuck pot roast (3 to 3½ pounds)

1 Stir the mushroom soup, soup mix, potatoes and carrots in a 4½-quart slow cooker. Add the beef and turn to coat.

2 Cover and cook on LOW for 8 to 9 hours* or until the beef is fork-tender.

Or on HIGH for 4 to 5 hours.

French Onion Burgers

MAKES 4 SERVINGS

PREP
5 MINUTES

COOK
20 MINUTES

1 **pound ground beef**

1 **can (10½ ounces) Campbell's® Condensed French Onion Soup**

4 **slices cheese**

4 **Pepperidge Farm® Classic Sandwich Buns, split**

You can also serve these burgers in a bowl atop a mound of hot mashed potatoes with some of the soup mixture poured over.

1 Shape the beef into **4** (½-inch-thick) burgers.

2 Heat a 10-inch skillet over medium-high heat. Add the burgers and cook until well browned on both sides. Remove the burgers from the skillet. Pour off any fat.

3 Stir the soup in the skillet and heat to a boil. Return the burgers to the skillet. Reduce the heat to low. Cover and cook for 5 minutes or until desired doneness. Top the burgers with the cheese and cook until the cheese is melted. Serve the burgers on the buns with the soup mixture for dipping.

Mushroom-Smothered Beef Burgers

MAKES 4 SERVINGS

1 can (10¾ ounces) Campbell's® Condensed Cream of Mushroom Soup (Regular *or* 98% Fat Free)

1 pound ground beef

⅓ cup Italian-seasoned dry bread crumbs

1 small onion, finely chopped (about ¼ cup)

1 egg, beaten

1 tablespoon vegetable oil

1 tablespoon Worcestershire sauce

2 tablespoons water

1½ cups sliced mushrooms (about 4 ounces)

PREP
15 MINUTES

COOK
25 MINUTES

1 Thoroughly mix ¼ **cup** soup, beef, bread crumbs, onion and egg in a large bowl. Shape the beef mixture **firmly** into 4 (½-inch-thick) burgers.

2 Heat the oil in a 10-inch skillet over medium-high heat. Add the burgers and cook until they're well browned on both sides. Pour off any fat.

3 Add the remaining soup, Worcestershire, water and mushrooms to the skillet and heat to a boil. Reduce the heat to low. Cover and cook for 10 minutes or until the burgers are cooked through.

tip

You can substitute ground turkey for the ground beef in this recipe.

Whether starting with pork chops,

sausage, or ham, you'll find dishes that

really satisfy everyone in your household.

pork

Slow-Cooked Pulled Pork Sandwiches

MAKES 12 SERVINGS

PREP
15 MINUTES

COOK
8 HOURS

STAND
10 MINUTES

1 **tablespoon vegetable oil**

1 **boneless pork shoulder roast (3½ to 4 pounds), netted *or* tied**

1 **can (10½ ounces) Campbell's® Condensed French Onion Soup**

1 **cup ketchup**

¼ **cup cider vinegar**

3 **tablespoons packed brown sugar**

12 **Pepperidge Farm® Sandwich Rolls, split**

1 Heat the oil in a 10-inch skillet over medium-high heat. Add the pork and cook until it's well browned on all sides.

2 Stir the soup, ketchup, vinegar and brown sugar in a 5-quart slow cooker. Add the pork and turn to coat.

3 Cover and cook on LOW for 8 to 9 hours* or until the pork is fork-tender.

4 Remove the pork from the cooker to a cutting board and let stand for 10 minutes. Using 2 forks, shred the pork. Return the pork to the cooker.

5 Spoon the pork and sauce mixture on the rolls.

Or on HIGH for 4 to 5 hours.

Apricot Glazed Pork Roast

MAKES 8 SERVINGS

PREP
5 MINUTES

COOK
8 HOURS

1 can (10½ ounces) Campbell's® Condensed Chicken Broth

1 jar (18 ounces) apricot preserves

1 large onion, chopped (about 1 cup)

2 tablespoons Dijon-style mustard

1 boneless pork loin roast (about 4 pounds)

1 Stir the broth, preserves, onion and mustard in a 3½-quart slow cooker. Add the pork to the cooker, cutting to fit, if needed, and turn to coat.

2 Cover and cook on LOW for 8 to 9 hours* or until the pork is fork-tender.

*Or on HIGH for 4 to 5 hours.

---

tip

For thicker sauce, mix **2 tablespoons** cornstarch and **2 tablespoons** water in a small bowl until smooth. Remove the pork from the cooker. Stir the cornstarch mixture in the cooker. Cover and cook on HIGH for 10 minutes or until the mixture boils and thickens.

Citrus Picante Roast Pork

MAKES 8 SERVINGS

PREP
15 MINUTES

BAKE
35 MINUTES

STAND
10 MINUTES

*You can try canned diced peaches **or** pineapple in this recipe, if you like.*

1 jar (11 ounces) Pace® Picante Sauce

1 can (11 ounces) Mandarin orange segments, drained

2 (1 pound *each*) pork tenderloins

1 teaspoon olive oil

2 tablespoons chopped fresh cilantro leaves

1 lime, cut into wedges

1 Heat the oven to 425°F. Stir the picante sauce and oranges in a small bowl.

2 Place the pork into a 3-quart shallow baking pan. Rub the pork with the oil. Pour the salsa mixture over the pork.

3 Bake for 35 minutes or until the pork is cooked through. Remove the pork from the pan and let stand for 10 minutes. Sprinkle with the cilantro and serve with the lime.

Creamy Pork Marsala with Fettuccine

MAKES 4 SERVINGS

PREP
5 MINUTES

COOK
25 MINUTES

1 **tablespoon olive oil**

4 **boneless pork chops, ³⁄₄-inch thick (about 1 pound)**

1 **cup sliced mushrooms (about 3 ounces)**

1 **clove garlic, minced**

1 **can (10³⁄₄ ounces) Campbell's® Condensed Cream of Mushroom Soup (Regular *or* 98% Fat Free)**

¹⁄₂ **cup milk**

2 **tablespoons dry Marsala wine**

8 **ounces spinach fettuccine, cooked and drained**

Marsalas can range from dry to sweet, so be sure to use a dry one for this recipe.

1 Heat the oil in a 10-inch skillet over medium-high heat. Add the pork and cook until it's well browned on both sides.

2 Reduce the heat to medium. Add the mushrooms and garlic to the skillet and cook until the mushrooms are tender.

3 Stir the soup, milk and wine in the skillet and heat to a boil. Reduce the heat to low. Cover and cook for 5 minutes or until the pork is cooked through. Serve the pork and sauce with the pasta.

Tuscan Sausage and Rigatoni

MAKES 8 SERVINGS

PREP
5 MINUTES

COOK
20 MINUTES

1 **pound sweet *or* hot Italian pork sausage, casing removed**

1 **package (8 ounces) sliced mushrooms**

1 **cup frozen peas**

2²/₃ **cups Prego® Traditional *or* Marinara Italian Sauce**

1 **package (16 ounces) large tube-shaped pasta (rigatoni) (about 6 cups), cooked and drained**

¹/₃ **cup grated Parmesan cheese**

1 Cook the sausage in a 10-inch skillet over medium-high heat until it's well browned, stirring often to separate the meat. Pour off any fat.

2 Stir the mushrooms and peas in the skillet. Cook for 5 minutes or until the mushrooms are tender, stirring often.

3 Stir the Italian sauce in the skillet. Reduce the heat to medium. Cook until the mixture is hot and bubbling, stirring occasionally.

4 Place the pasta into a large serving bowl. Pour the sausage mixture over the pasta and toss to coat. Top with the cheese.

Tomato & Onion Pork Chops with Cannellini Beans

MAKES 6 SERVINGS

PREP
10 MINUTES

COOK
45 MINUTES

¼ **cup olive oil**

6 **boneless pork chops, ½-inch thick *each* (about
1½ pounds)**

3 **garlic cloves, minced**

1 **large onion, finely chopped (about 1 cup)**

3 **cups Prego® Chunky Garden Tomato, Onion & Garlic
Italian Sauce**

1 **can (about 15 ounces) white kidney beans (cannellini)
or navy beans, undrained**

1 **package (10 ounces) Pepperidge Farm® Mozzarella
Garlic Bread**

2 **tablespoons chopped fresh basil leaves**

1 Heat **3 tablespoons** of the oil in a 6-quart saucepot over
medium-high heat. Add the pork and cook until it's well
browned on both sides. Remove the pork from the saucepot.

2 Heat the remaining oil in the saucepot over medium heat.
Add the garlic and onion and cook for 3 minutes or until the
onion is tender.

3 Preheat the oven to 400°F. for the bread.

4 Return the pork to the saucepot. Stir the Italian sauce in the
saucepot and heat to a boil. Reduce the heat to low. Cover
and cook for 20 minutes or until the pork is cooked through.
Stir in the beans and cook until the mixture is hot and bubbling.

5 Meanwhile, bake the bread according to the package
directions.

6 Sprinkle the pork mixture with the basil. Cut the bread into
2-inch diagonal slices. Serve the bread with the pork.

Glorified Onion Pork Chops

MAKES 6 SERVINGS

PREP
10 MINUTES

COOK
25 MINUTES

1 **tablespoon vegetable oil**

6 **bone-in pork chops, $1/2$-inch thick (about 3 pounds)**

1 **medium onion, sliced (about $1/2$ cup)**

1 **can (10$3/4$ ounces) Campbell's® Condensed Cream of Celery Soup (Regular *or* 98% Fat Free)**

$1/2$ **cup water**

1 Heat the oil in a 12-inch skillet over medium-high heat. Add the pork and cook until well browned on both sides.

2 Add the onion and cook until the onion is tender, stirring occasionally. Stir in the soup and water and heat to a boil. Reduce the heat to low. Cook for 5 minutes or until the pork is cooked through.

Slow Cooker Golden Mushroom Pork & Apples

MAKES 8 SERVINGS

PREP
10 MINUTES

COOK
8 HOURS

2 **cans (10¾ ounces *each*) Campbell's® Condensed Golden Mushroom Soup**

½ **cup water**

1 **tablespoon packed brown sugar**

1 **tablespoon Worcestershire sauce**

1 **teaspoon dried thyme leaves, crushed**

8 **boneless pork chops, ¾-inch thick (about 2 pounds)**

4 **large Granny Smith apples, sliced**

2 **large onions, sliced (about 2 cups)**

1 Stir the soup, water, brown sugar, Worcestershire and thyme in a 3½-quart slow cooker. Add the pork, apples and onions.

2 Cover and cook on LOW for 8 to 9 hours* or until the pork is cooked through.

Or on HIGH for 4 to 5 hours.

Honey-Barbecued Ribs

MAKES 4 SERVINGS

PREP
10 MINUTES

COOK
1 HOUR

4 **pork spareribs, cut into serving-sized pieces**

1 **can (10½ ounces) Campbell's® Condensed French Onion Soup**

¾ **cup ketchup**

⅓ **cup honey**

½ **teaspoon garlic powder**

½ **teaspoon ground black pepper**

1 Place the ribs into a 6-quart saucepot and add water to cover. Heat over medium-high heat to a boil. Reduce the heat to low. Cover and cook for 30 minutes or until the meat is tender. Drain the ribs well in a colander.

2 Heat the soup, ketchup, honey, garlic powder and black pepper in a 2-quart saucepan over medium-high heat to a boil. Reduce the heat to low. Cook for 5 minutes.

3 Lightly oil the grill rack and heat the grill to medium. Grill the ribs for 20 minutes or until they're cooked through, turning and brushing often with the soup mixture.

Pork with Mushroom Dijon Sauce

MAKES 4 SERVINGS

- **4 boneless pork chops, ³/₄-inch thick (about 1 pound)**
- **¹/₂ teaspoon lemon pepper seasoning**
- **1 tablespoon vegetable oil**
- **1 cup sliced mushrooms (about 3 ounces)**
- **1 can (10³/₄ ounces) Campbell's® Condensed Cream of Mushroom Soup (Regular or 98% Fat Free)**
- **¹/₄ cup milk**
- **2 tablespoons Chablis or other dry white wine**
- **1 tablespoon Dijon-style mustard**

PREP
10 MINUTES
COOK
30 MINUTES

1 Season the pork with the lemon pepper.

2 Heat the oil in a 10-inch skillet over medium-high heat. Add the pork and cook until it's well browned on both sides. Remove the pork from the skillet.

3 Add the mushrooms to the skillet. Reduce the heat to medium. Cook until the mushrooms are tender, stirring occasionally.

4 Stir the soup, milk, wine and mustard in the skillet and heat to a boil. Return the pork to the skillet. Reduce the heat to low. Cover and cook for 10 minutes or until the pork is cooked through.

Seafood and fish entrées found here

are just as tasty as you'll find in restaurants.

fish & seafood

Shrimp Scampi with Garlic Bread

MAKES 4 SERVINGS

PREP
25 MINUTES

MARINATE
30 MINUTES

COOK
25 MINUTES

1 **tablespoon lemon zest**

5 **tablespoons olive oil**

4 **teaspoons chopped fresh oregano leaves**

4 **cloves garlic, minced**

½ **teaspoon ground black pepper**

24 **fresh *or* frozen jumbo shrimp, shelled and deveined**

2 **tablespoons lemon juice**

3 **tablespoons unsalted butter**

1 **package (10 ounces) Pepperidge Farm® Garlic Bread**

Sprigs fresh oregano leaves

1 Stir the lemon zest, **3 tablespoons** oil, **1 teaspoon** oregano, **2 teaspoons** garlic and the black pepper in a shallow nonmetallic dish or a gallon-size resealable plastic bag. Add the shrimp and turn to coat. Cover the dish or seal the bag and refrigerate for 30 minutes.

2 Heat the remaining oil in an 8-inch skillet over medium heat. Add the remaining garlic and cook and stir until tender. Stir in the lemon juice and remaining oregano. Remove the skillet from the heat. Add the butter and stir until the butter is melted. Keep warm.

3 Prepare the bread according to the package directions. Cut each bread half diagonally into **6** (½-inch thick) slices.

4 Heat the broiler. Place the bread slices onto a baking sheet. Broil 7 inches from the heat for 2 minutes or until the bread is toasted on both sides.

5 Remove the shrimp from the marinade and discard the marinade. Heat the broiler. Place the shrimp on a rack in a broiler pan. Broil the shrimp 6 inches from the heat for 5 minutes or until the shrimp are cooked through, turning the shrimp over once halfway through broiling.

6 Place the shrimp onto a serving platter. Drizzle with the butter mixture. Serve with the bread. Garnish with the oregano sprigs.

Poached Halibut with Pineapple Salsa

MAKES 4 SERVINGS

PREP
10 MINUTES

COOK
15 MINUTES

1 **can (about 15 ounces) pineapple chunks in juice, undrained**

1 **seedless cucumber, peeled and diced (about 1²/₃ cups)**

1 **medium red pepper, chopped (about ³/₄ cup)**

2 **tablespoons chopped red onion**

1 **teaspoon white wine vinegar**

1 **teaspoon hot pepper sauce (optional)**

1³/₄ **cups Swanson® Chicken Stock**

¹/₄ **cup white wine**

4 **halibut fillets (about 1¹/₂ pounds)**

1 Drain the pineapple and reserve ²/₃ **cup** juice.

2 Stir the pineapple chunks, cucumber, red pepper, red onion, vinegar and hot pepper sauce, if desired, in a medium bowl.

3 Heat the stock, wine and reserved pineapple juice in a 12-inch skillet over medium-high heat to a boil. Add the fish to the skillet. Reduce the heat to low. Cover and cook for 10 minutes or until the fish flakes easily when tested with a fork. Serve the fish with the pineapple salsa.

Balsamic Glazed Salmon

MAKES 8 SERVINGS

PREP
5 MINUTES

BAKE
15 MINUTES

COOK
5 MINUTES

8 **fresh salmon fillets, ³/₄-inch thick (about 1¹/₂ pounds)**

Freshly ground black pepper

3 **tablespoons olive oil**

4¹/₂ **teaspoons cornstarch**

1³/₄ **cups Swanson® Chicken Stock**

3 **tablespoons balsamic vinegar**

1 **tablespoon brown sugar**

1 **tablespoon orange juice**

1 **teaspoon grated orange zest**

Orange slices for garnish

1 Place the salmon in an 11×8-inch (2-quart) shallow baking dish. Sprinkle with black pepper and drizzle with oil. Bake at 350°F. for 15 minutes or until the fish flakes easily when tested with a fork.

2 Stir the cornstarch, stock, vinegar, brown sugar, orange juice and orange zest in a 2-quart saucepan over high heat to a boil. Cook and stir until the mixture boils and thickens.

3 Place the salmon on a serving platter and serve with the sauce. Garnish with the orange slices.

When grating citrus fruits, you'll want to avoid rubbing too deeply into the peel. There's a white layer between the outer peel and the flesh, called the pith, which can be bitter.

Crusted Tilapia Florentine

MAKES 4 SERVINGS

PREP
10 MINUTES

COOK
15 MINUTES

1 **egg**

2 **teaspoons water**

1 **cup Italian-seasoned dry bread crumbs**

4 **fresh tilapia fillets (about 4 ounces *each*)**

2 **tablespoons olive oil**

2⅔ **cups Prego® Traditional Italian Sauce**

2 **cups frozen chopped spinach**

Hot cooked noodles

1 Beat the egg and water with a fork in a shallow dish. Place the bread crumbs on a plate. Dip the fish in the egg mixture, then coat with the bread crumbs.

2 Heat the oil in a 12-inch skillet over medium-high heat. Add the fish and cook for 8 minutes, turning once or until the fish flakes easily when tested with a fork. Remove the fish and keep warm.

3 Stir the Italian sauce and spinach into the skillet. Heat to a boil. Reduce the heat to medium. Cook for 2 minutes or until the spinach is wilted. Serve the sauce over the fish. Serve with the noodles.

Halibut with Beans and Spinach

MAKES 4 SERVINGS

PREP
10 MINUTES

COOK
15 MINUTES

2 tablespoons olive oil

1 teaspoon minced garlic

4 fresh halibut fillets (6 ounces *each*)

1¾ cups Swanson® Chicken Stock

2 tablespoons lemon juice

2 cups frozen cut leaf spinach

1 can (about 15 ounces) Great Northern beans, rinsed
and drained

Generous dash crushed red pepper

1 Stir **1 tablespoon** of the oil and garlic in a shallow dish. Add the halibut and turn to coat.

2 Heat the remaining oil in a 10-inch skillet over medium-high heat. Add the fish and cook for about 4 minutes, turning halfway through cooking. Remove the fish with a spatula.

3 Stir the stock and lemon juice into the skillet. Heat to a boil. Add the spinach, beans and red pepper. Return the fish to the skillet. Reduce the heat to low. Cover and cook for 2 minutes or until the fish flakes easily when tested with a fork and the mixture is hot and bubbling.

Grilled Fish Steaks with Chunky Tomato Sauce

MAKES 6 SERVINGS

| PREP |
| 15 MINUTES |
| GRILL |
| 10 MINUTES |

Vegetable cooking spray

½ **cup chopped celery (about 1 stalk)**

½ **cup chopped green pepper (about 1 small)**

½ **cup chopped onion (about 1 medium)**

½ **teaspoon dried thyme leaves, crushed**

¼ **teaspoon garlic powder *or* 2 cloves garlic, minced**

1 **can (10¾ ounces) Campbell's® Healthy Request® Condensed Tomato Soup**

2 **tablespoons lemon juice**

⅛ **teaspoon hot pepper sauce (optional)**

6 **swordfish steaks, 1-inch thick**

1 Spray a 2-quart saucepan with vegetable cooking spray. Heat over medium heat for 1 minute. Add the celery, green pepper, onion, thyme and garlic powder and cook until tender, stirring often.

2 Stir in the soup, lemon juice and hot pepper sauce, if desired. Heat through, stirring occasionally.

3 Lightly oil the grill rack and heat the grill to medium. Grill the fish uncovered for 10 minutes or until the fish flakes easily when tested with a fork, turning once during cooking. Serve the sauce over the fish.

Classic Tuna Noodle Casserole

MAKES 4 SERVINGS

PREP
10 MINUTES

BAKE
25 MINUTES

1 can (10¾ ounces) Campbell's® Condensed Cream of Celery Soup (Regular *or* 98% Fat Free)

½ cup milk

1 cup cooked peas

2 tablespoons chopped pimientos

2 cans (about 6 ounces *each*) tuna, drained and flaked

2 cups hot cooked medium egg noodles

2 tablespoons dry bread crumbs

1 tablespoon butter, melted

1 Heat the oven to 400°F. Stir the soup, milk, peas, pimientos, tuna and noodles in a 1½-quart baking dish. Stir the bread crumbs and butter in a small bowl.

2 Bake for 20 minutes or until the tuna mixture is hot and bubbling. Stir the tuna mixture. Sprinkle with the bread crumb mixture.

3 Bake for 5 minutes or until the bread crumbs are golden brown.

Substitute Campbell's® Condensed Cream of Mushroom Soup for the Cream of Celery.

To melt the butter, remove the wrapper and place the butter in a microwavable cup. Cover and microwave on HIGH for 30 seconds.

Grilled Skewered Shrimp

MAKES 6 SERVINGS

PREP 20 MINUTES **GRILL** 10 MINUTES

⅔ **cup Pace® Picante Sauce**

1 **can (about 8 ounces) tomato sauce**

3 **tablespoons packed brown sugar**

2 **tablespoons lemon juice**

1½ **pounds large shrimp, peeled and deveined**

1 Stir the picante sauce, tomato sauce, brown sugar and lemon juice in a large bowl. Add the shrimp and toss to coat.

2 Thread the shrimp on **12** skewers.

3 Lightly oil the grill rack and heat the grill to medium. Grill the shrimp for 10 minutes or until they're cooked through, turning and brushing often with the picante sauce mixture. Discard any remaining picante sauce mixture.

For even easier preparation, you can buy frozen large shrimp already peeled and deveined. Just thaw and use instead of the fresh shrimp.

Fish Stuffing Bake

MAKES 6 SERVINGS

PREP
30 MINUTES

BAKE
15 MINUTES

1 **cup water***

¼ **cup (½ stick) butter**

2 **medium carrots, sliced (about 1 cup)**

1 **small green pepper, chopped (about ½ cup)**

4 **cups Pepperidge Farm® Herb Seasoned Stuffing**

6 **fresh *or* thawed frozen firm white fish fillets (cod, haddock *or* halibut) (about 1½ pounds)**

1 **tablespoon lemon juice**

1 **tablespoon chopped fresh parsley *or* 1 teaspoon dried parsley flakes**

For moister stuffing increase the water to 1½ cups.

1 Heat the water, **2 tablespoons** butter, carrots and pepper in a 3-quart saucepan over medium-high heat to a boil. Remove the saucepan from the heat. Add the stuffing and mix lightly.

2 Spoon the stuffing across the center of a 3-quart shallow baking dish. Arrange the fish on each side of the stuffing.

3 Heat the remaining butter in an 8-inch skillet over medium heat until it's melted. Stir in the lemon juice and parsley. Spoon the butter mixture over the fish.

4 Bake at 400°F. for 15 minutes or until the fish flakes easily when tested with a fork.

Roasted Garlic & Herb Shrimp with Spaghetti

MAKES 4 SERVINGS

2 **tablespoons olive oil**

3 **cloves garlic, crushed**

3 **cups Prego® Roasted Garlic & Herb Italian Sauce**

½ **teaspoon crushed red pepper**

1 **pound fresh *or* thawed frozen medium shrimp, peeled and deveined**

1 **package (10 ounces) Pepperidge Farm® Garlic Bread**

1 **package (16 ounces) spaghetti, cooked and drained (about 8 cups)**

3 **tablespoons minced fresh Italian parsley**

PREP
20 MINUTES

COOK
15 MINUTES

1 Heat the oven to 400°F. for the bread.

2 Heat the oil in a 12-inch skillet over medium heat. Add the garlic and cook until it's golden.

3 Stir the Italian sauce and red pepper in the skillet and heat to a boil. Reduce the heat to low. Add the shrimp and cook for 5 minutes or until they're cooked through.

4 Meanwhile, bake the bread according to the package directions.

5 Toss the spaghetti with the shrimp mixture. Sprinkle with the parsley. Cut the bread into 2-inch diagonal slices. Serve the bread with the spaghetti mixture.

Packed with punch, these recipes are proof

positive that meatless dishes taste great!

vegetarian
plates

Penne with Creamy Vodka Sauce

MAKES 4 SERVINGS

PREP

15 MINUTES

COOK

10 MINUTES

5½ **cups Prego® Chunky Garden Tomato, Onion & Garlic Italian Sauce**

¼ **cup vodka**

⅓ **cup chopped fresh basil leaves**

¼ **teaspoon crushed red pepper**

½ **cup heavy cream**

9 **cups medium tube-shaped pasta (penne), cooked and drained**

Grated Parmesan cheese

1 Heat the Italian sauce, vodka, basil and pepper in a 3-quart saucepan over medium heat until the mixture comes to a boil. Remove from the heat and stir in the cream.

2 Put the pasta in a large serving bowl. Pour the sauce mixture over the pasta. Toss to coat.

3 Sprinkle with the cheese.

Three Cheese Baked Ziti with Spinach

MAKES 6 SERVINGS

PREP
15 MINUTES

BAKE
30 MINUTES

1 package (16 ounces) *uncooked* medium tube-shaped pasta (ziti)

1 bag (6 ounces) baby spinach, washed (about 4 cups)

1 jar (1 pound 9 ounces) Prego® Marinara Italian Sauce

1 cup ricotta cheese

4 ounces shredded mozzarella cheese (about 1 cup)

¾ cup grated Parmesan cheese

½ teaspoon garlic powder

¼ teaspoon ground black pepper

Save valuable time by putting together the casserole a day or less in advance, covering and refrigerating it to bake later to everyone's delight.

1 Prepare the pasta according to the package directions. Add the spinach during the last minute of the cooking time. Drain the pasta and spinach well in a colander. Return them to the saucepot.

2 Stir the Italian sauce, ricotta, ½ **cup** of the mozzarella cheese, ½ **cup** of the Parmesan cheese, garlic powder and black pepper into the pasta mixture. Spoon the pasta mixture into a 13×9×2-inch shallow baking dish. Sprinkle with the remaining mozzarella and Parmesan cheeses.

3 Bake at 350°F. for 30 minutes or it's until hot and bubbling.

Broccoli & Cheese Casserole

MAKES 6 SERVINGS

PREP
10 MINUTES

BAKE
30 MINUTES

1 can (10¾ ounces) Campbell's® Condensed Cream of Mushroom Soup (Regular *or* 98% Fat Free)

½ cup milk

2 teaspoons yellow mustard

1 bag (16 ounces) frozen broccoli florets, thawed

1 cup shredded Cheddar cheese (4 ounces)

⅓ cup dry bread crumbs

2 teaspoons butter, melted

1 Stir the soup, milk, mustard, broccoli and cheese in a 1½-quart casserole.

2 Stir the bread crumbs and butter in a small bowl. Sprinkle the crumb mixture over the broccoli mixture.

3 Bake at 350°F. for 30 minutes or until the mixture is hot and bubbling.

Rice Is Nice: Add **2 cups** cooked white rice to the broccoli mixture before baking.

Cheese Change-Up: Substitute mozzarella cheese for the Cheddar.

Ratatouille Tart

MAKES 8 SERVINGS

THAW
40 MINUTES

PREP
50 MINUTES

BAKE
1 HOUR
15 MINUTES

½ **of a 17.3-ounce package Pepperidge Farm® Puff Pastry Sheets (1 sheet), thawed**

¼ **cup olive oil**

1 **medium eggplant, peeled and cut into ½-inch cubes (about 5½ cups)**

1 **medium onion, chopped (about ½ cup)**

3 **cloves garlic, minced**

2 **medium zucchini, peeled and diced (about 2 cups)**

1 **medium green pepper, diced (about 1 cup)**

1 **teaspoon dried oregano leaves, crushed**

½ **teaspoon ground black pepper**

1 **can (8 ounces) tomato sauce**

1 **tablespoon tomato paste**

1 **tablespoon red wine vinegar**

All-purpose flour

5 **small Italian plum tomatoes, sliced**

2 **small zucchini, sliced (about 2 cups)**

1 **tablespoon dry bread crumbs**

1 Heat the oven to 350°F.

2 Heat the oil in a 12-inch skillet over medium heat. Add the eggplant, onion and garlic and cook for 5 minutes, stirring occasionally. Add the zucchini and green pepper. Cook until the vegetables are tender. Season with the oregano and black pepper.

3 Stir the tomato sauce, tomato paste and vinegar in the skillet. Cook for 5 minutes.

4 Sprinkle the flour on the work surface. Unfold the pastry sheet on the work surface. Roll the pastry sheet into a 12-inch square. Cut off the corners to make a circle. Press the pastry into the bottom and up the sides of a 10-inch tart pan with a removable bottom. Trim off the excess pastry. Prick the pastry thoroughly with a fork. Place a piece of aluminum foil onto the pastry. Add pie weights or dried beans.

5 Bake for 15 minutes or until the pastry is golden brown. Remove the foil and weights. Let the pastry cool in the pan on a wire rack for 10 minutes.

6 Spoon the eggplant mixture into the crust. Arrange the tomatoes and zucchini in concentric circles to completely cover the eggplant mixture. Sprinkle with the bread crumbs.

7 Bake for 1 hour or until the zucchini and tomatoes are browned.

Ratatouille-Stuffed Portobello Mushrooms: Omit the puff pastry. Prepare the eggplant filling as directed above. Cook 5 to 6 portobello mushrooms top-side down in **1 tablespoon** olive oil in a 12-inch skillet over medium-high heat for 10 minutes or until golden brown. Turn over and cook about 5 minutes more or until tender. Divide the eggplant mixture among the mushrooms. Sprinkle with ¼ **cup** chopped fresh parsley.

Broccoli and Pasta Bianco

MAKES 8 SERVINGS

PREP
20 MINUTES

BAKE
25 MINUTES

6 cups *uncooked* penne pasta

4 cups fresh *or* frozen broccoli florets

1 can (10¾ ounces) Campbell's® Condensed Cream of Mushroom Soup (Regular *or* 98% Fat Free)

1½ cups milk

½ teaspoon ground black pepper

1½ cups shredded mozzarella cheese (about 6 ounces)

¼ cup shredded Parmesan cheese

1 Heat the oven to 350°F.

2 Cook the pasta according to the package directions. Add the broccoli for the last 4 minutes of cooking time. Drain the pasta mixture well in a colander.

3 Stir the soup, milk and black pepper in a 2-quart shallow baking dish. Stir in the pasta mixture, ¾ **cup** mozzarella cheese and **2 tablespoons** Parmesan cheese. Top with the remaining mozzarella and Parmesan cheeses.

4 Bake for 25 minutes or until the pasta mixture is hot and bubbling and the cheese is melted.

Creamy white pastas like this one taste great with the tang and heat of crushed red pepper flakes. Serve it on the side.

Greek Rice Bake

MAKES 6 SERVINGS

PREP
15 MINUTES

BAKE
40 MINUTES

STAND
5 MINUTES

1 **can (10¾ ounces) Campbell's® Condensed Cream of Mushroom Soup (Regular *or* 98% Fat Free)**

½ **cup water**

1 **can (about 14.5 ounces) diced tomatoes, undrained**

1 **jar (6 ounces) marinated artichoke hearts, drained and cut in half**

2 **portobello mushrooms, coarsely chopped (about 2 cups)**

¾ **cup *uncooked* quick-cooking brown rice**

1 **can (about 15 ounces) small white beans, rinsed and drained**

3 **to 4 tablespoons crumbled feta cheese**

1 Heat the oven to 400°F. Stir the soup, water, tomatoes, artichokes, mushrooms, rice and beans in a 2-quart casserole. Cover the casserole.

2 Bake for 40 minutes or until the rice is tender. Stir the rice mixture. Let stand for 5 minutes. Sprinkle with the cheese before serving.

Different brands of quick-cooking brown rice cook differently, so the bake time for this recipe may be slightly longer or shorter than indicated.

Baked Macaroni and Cheese

MAKES 4 SERVINGS

PREP
20 MINUTES

BAKE
20 MINUTES

1 can (10¾ ounces) Campbell's® Condensed Cheddar Cheese Soup

½ soup can milk

⅛ teaspoon ground black pepper

2 cups corkscrew-shaped pasta (rotini) *or* shell-shaped pasta, cooked and drained

1 tablespoon dry bread crumbs

2 teaspoons butter, melted

1 Stir the soup, milk, black pepper and pasta in a 1-quart baking dish.

2 Stir the bread crumbs and butter in a small bowl. Sprinkle the bread crumb mixture over the pasta mixture.

3 Bake at 400°F. for 20 minutes or until the pasta mixture is hot and bubbling.

Hearty Vegetarian Chili

MAKES 4 SERVINGS

2 **tablespoons vegetable oil**

1 **large onion, chopped (about 1 cup)**

1 **small green pepper, chopped (about ½ cup)**

¼ **teaspoon garlic powder *or* 2 small garlic cloves, minced**

1 **tablespoon chili powder**

½ **teaspoon ground cumin**

2½ **cups V8® 100% Vegetable Juice**

1 **can (about 15 ounces) black beans *or* red kidney beans, rinsed and drained**

1 **can (about 15 ounces) pinto beans, rinsed and drained**

PREP
10 MINUTES

COOK
20 MINUTES

1 Heat the oil in a 2-quart saucepan over medium heat. Add the onion, pepper, garlic powder, chili powder and cumin and cook until the vegetables are tender, stirring occasionally.

2 Stir the vegetable juice in the saucepan and heat to a boil. Reduce the heat to low. Cook for 5 minutes.

3 Stir in the beans and cook until the mixture is hot and bubbling.

Zucchini, Tomato & Mozzarella Tart

MAKES 8 SERVINGS

THAW
40 MINUTES

PREP
20 MINUTES

BAKE
45 MINUTES

COOL
20 MINUTES

½ **of a 17.3-ounce package Pepperidge Farm® Puff Pastry Sheets (1 sheet), thawed**

1½ **cups shredded mozzarella cheese (about 6 ounces)**

¾ **cup freshly grated Parmesan cheese**

½ **cup thinly sliced fresh basil leaves**

2 **medium green onions, chopped (about ¼ cup)**

1 **tablespoon chopped fresh oregano leaves**

2 **small zucchini, sliced (about 2 cups)**

3 **Italian plum tomatoes, thinly sliced**

2 **eggs**

1 **cup half-and-half**

¼ **teaspoon ground black pepper**

1 Heat the oven to 400°F.

2 Unfold the pastry sheet on a lightly floured surface. Roll the pastry sheet into a 13-inch square. Cut off the corners to make a circle. Press the pastry into the bottom and up the sides of a 9-inch springform pan, leaving the excess pastry draped over the sides of the pan.

3 Layer the mozzarella cheese, ½ cup Parmesan cheese, basil, green onions and oregano in the pan. Arrange the zucchini and tomatoes in concentric circles on top.

4 Beat the eggs, half-and-half and black pepper in a medium bowl with a fork or whisk. Pour the egg mixture over the vegetables. Sprinkle with the remaining Parmesan cheese. Fold the excess pastry in over the filling.

5 Bake for 45 minutes or until set. Let the tart cool in the pan on a wire rack for 20 minutes.

Creamy 3-Cheese Pasta

MAKES 4 SERVINGS

1   **can (10¾ ounces) Campbell's® Condensed Cream of Mushroom Soup (Regular *or* 98% Fat Free)**

1   **package (8 ounces) shredded two-cheese blend (about 2 cups)**

⅓   **cup grated Parmesan cheese**

1   **cup milk**

¼   **teaspoon ground black pepper**

3   **cups corkscrew-shaped pasta (rotini), cooked and drained**

PREP
20 MINUTES

BAKE
20 MINUTES

1 Stir the soup, cheeses, milk and black pepper in a 1½-quart casserole. Stir in the pasta.

2 Bake at 400°F. for 20 minutes or until the pasta mixture is hot and bubbling.

Simple sides make an ordinary weeknight

dinner turn into a memorable meal.

side dishes

Green Bean Casserole

MAKES 5 SERVINGS

PREP
10 MINUTES

BAKE
30 MINUTES

1 can (10¾ ounces) Campbell's® Condensed Cream of Mushroom Soup (Regular *or* 98% Fat Free)

½ cup milk

1 teaspoon soy sauce

Dash ground black pepper

2 packages (10 ounces *each*) frozen cut green beans, cooked and drained

1 can (2.8 ounces) French fried onions (1⅓ cups)

1 Stir the soup, milk, soy sauce, black pepper, green beans and ⅔ **cup** onions in a 1½-quart casserole.

2 Bake at 350°F. for 25 minutes or until hot. Stir the green bean mixture.

3 Sprinkle the remaining onions over the green bean mixture. Bake for 5 minutes more or until onions are golden brown.

tip

*You can also make this classic side dish with fresh **or** canned green beans. You will need either 1½ **pounds** fresh green beans, cut into 1-inch pieces, cooked and drained, **or 2 cans** (about 16 ounces **each**) cut green beans, drained, for the frozen green beans.*

White & Wild Rice Pilaf

MAKES 8 SERVINGS

PREP
20 MINUTES

COOK
50 MINUTES

1 **tablespoon olive oil**

1 **large onion, chopped (about 1 cup)**

2 **large carrots, chopped (about 1 cup)**

2 **stalks celery, sliced (about 1 cup)**

2 **cloves garlic, minced**

3½ **cups Swanson® Vegetable Broth (Regular *or* Certified Organic)**

½ **cup *uncooked* wild rice**

1 **cup *uncooked* regular long-grain white rice**

2 **tablespoons chopped fresh parsley**

1 Heat the oil in a 12-inch nonstick skillet over medium heat. Add the onion, carrots, celery and garlic and cook until the vegetables are tender.

2 Stir the broth and wild rice in the skillet and heat to a boil. Reduce the heat to low. Cover and cook for 25 minutes.

3 Stir in the white rice. Cover and cook for 20 minutes or until the rice is tender. Sprinkle with the parsley.

tip

*Wild rice is a relatively expensive ingredient, but a little goes a long way. The ½ **cup** in this recipe lends texture and a rich nutty flavor.*

Broccoli & Noodles Supreme

MAKES 5 SERVINGS

PREP
10 MINUTES

COOK
25 MINUTES

3 cups *uncooked* medium egg noodles

2 cups fresh *or* frozen broccoli florets

1 can (10 ¾ ounces) Campbell's® Condensed Cream
  of Chicken Soup (Regular *or* 98% Fat Free)

½ cup sour cream

⅓ cup grated Parmesan cheese

⅛ teaspoon ground black pepper

1 Cook the noodles according to the package directions. Add the broccoli for the last 5 minutes of cooking time. Drain the noodle mixture well in a colander. Return the noodle mixture to the saucepan.

2 Stir the soup, sour cream, cheese and black pepper in the saucepan and cook over medium heat until the mixture is hot and bubbling, stirring often.

Sausage & Apple Stuffing

MAKES 8 SERVINGS

PREP
15 MINUTES

COOK
10 MINUTES

1¾ cups Swanson® Chicken Broth (Regular, Natural Goodness® *or* Certified Organic)

Generous dash ground black pepper

1 **stalk celery, coarsely chopped (about ½ cup)**

1 **small onion, coarsely chopped (about ¼ cup)**

½ **red apple, chopped**

½ **green apple, chopped**

½ **pound bulk pork sausage, cooked and crumbled**

2 **cups Pepperidge Farm® Herb Seasoned Stuffing**

2 **cups Pepperidge Farm® Corn Bread Stuffing**

1 Heat the broth, black pepper, celery, onion and apples in a 3-quart saucepan over medium-high heat to a boil. Reduce the heat to low. Cover and cook for 5 minutes or until the vegetables are tender.

2 Add the sausage and stuffing and stir lightly to coat.

*For an Interesting Twist: Omit the apples. Add ½ **teaspoon** chili powder. Use ½ **pound** smoked chorizo sausage, casing removed, and cut into ½-inch pieces for the pork sausage.*

Savory Vegetable Stuffing Bake

MAKES 6 SERVINGS

PREP
20 MINUTES

BAKE
30 MINUTES

¼ **pound bulk pork sausage**

1 **large onion, chopped (about 1 cup)**

½ **teaspoon dried thyme leaves, crushed**

1 **can (10¾ ounces) Campbell's® Condensed Cream of Celery Soup (Regular *or* 98% Fat Free)**

1 **can (about 8 ounces) stewed tomatoes**

2 **cups frozen vegetable combination (broccoli, corn, red pepper)**

3 **cups Pepperidge Farm® Herb Seasoned Stuffing**

1 Cook the sausage, onion and thyme in a 12-inch skillet over medium-high heat until the sausage is browned, stirring frequently to separate the meat. Pour off any fat.

2 Stir the soup, tomatoes and vegetables in the skillet. Heat to a boil. Remove the skillet from the heat. Add the stuffing and stir lightly to coat. Spoon into a 1½-quart casserole.

3 Bake at 350°F. for 30 minutes or until it's hot and bubbling.

Mediterranean Chop Salad

MAKES 8 SERVINGS

PREP
25 MINUTES

3 **stalks celery, sliced (about 1½ cups) *or* 1 cup sliced fennel**

1 **cup chopped roasted red *or* yellow pepper**

1 **large seedless cucumber, peeled and chopped (about 1⅔ cups)**

½ **cup chopped pitted ripe olives**

½ **cup prepared balsamic vinaigrette salad dressing**

1 **package (12 ounces) hearts of romaine, chopped (about 8 cups)**

1 **box (5.5 ounces) Pepperidge Farm® Seasoned Croutons (your favorite variety)**

Freshly ground black pepper

Parmesan cheese shavings

1 Stir the celery, red pepper, cucumber, olives and dressing in a large serving bowl. Cover and refrigerate until serving time.

2 Add the lettuce and croutons to the dressing mixture just before serving and toss to coat. Season with the black pepper. Top with the cheese.

Broth Simmered Rice

MAKES 4 SERVINGS

PREP
5 MINUTES

COOK
25 MINUTES

1¾ cups Swanson® Chicken Broth (Regular, Natural Goodness® *or* Certified Organic)

¾ cup *uncooked* regular long-grain white rice

1 Heat the broth in a 2-quart saucepan over medium-high heat to a boil.

2 Stir in the rice. Reduce the heat to low. Cover and cook for 20 minutes or until the rice is tender.

Florentine Simmered Rice: Add **1 teaspoon** dried Italian seasoning to broth. Add **1 cup** chopped spinach with rice. Stir in ½ **cup** grated Parmesan cheese before serving. Serve with additional cheese.

This recipe will work with any variety of Swanson® Broth.

Herb Grilled Vegetables

MAKES 6 SERVINGS

½ cup Swanson® Chicken Broth (Regular, Natural Goodness® or Certified Organic)

½ teaspoon dried thyme leaves, crushed

⅛ teaspoon ground black pepper

1 large red onion, thickly sliced (about 1 cup)

1 large red *or* green pepper, cut into wide strips (about 2 cups)

1 medium zucchini *or* yellow squash, thickly sliced (about 1½ cups)

2 cups large mushrooms

1 Stir the broth, thyme and black pepper in a small bowl. Brush the vegetables with the broth mixture.

2 Lightly oil the grill rack and heat the grill to medium. Grill the vegetables for 10 minutes or until they're tender-crisp, turning over once during cooking and brushing often with the broth mixture.

PREP
10 MINUTES

GRILL
10 MINUTES

tips

A grilling basket is handy for grilling smaller foods like these veggies. Just place the vegetables in a single layer in the basket, close and place on the grill. You can baste the vegetables right in the basket, and flip the basket to grill the other side.

Swanson® Vegetable Broth may be used instead of Swanson® Chicken Broth for a vegetarian dish.

Moist & Savory Stuffing

MAKES 10 SERVINGS

PREP
10 MINUTES

COOK
10 MINUTES

BAKE
30 MINUTES

2½ **cups Swanson® Chicken Broth (Regular, Natural Goodness® *or* Certified Organic)**

Generous dash ground black pepper

2 **stalks celery, coarsely chopped (about 1 cup)**

1 **large onion, coarsely chopped (about 1 cup)**

1 **package (16 ounces) Pepperidge Farm® Herb Seasoned Stuffing**

tip

For crunchier stuffing, bake the casserole uncovered.

1 Heat the broth, black pepper, celery and onion in a 3-quart saucepan over medium-high heat to a boil. Reduce the heat to low. Cover and cook for 5 minutes or until the vegetables are tender, stirring often. Remove the saucepan from the heat. Add the stuffing and mix lightly.

2 Spoon the stuffing mixture into a greased 3-quart shallow baking dish. Cover the baking dish.

3 Bake at 350°F. for 30 minutes or until the stuffing is hot.

Cranberry & Pecan Stuffing: Stir ½ **cup each** dried cranberries **and** chopped pecans into the stuffing mixture.

Sausage & Mushroom Stuffing: Add **1 cup** sliced mushrooms to the vegetables during cooking. Stir ½ **pound** pork sausage, cooked and crumbled, into the stuffing mixture before baking.

Ultra Creamy Mashed Potatoes

MAKES 6 SERVINGS

3½ cups Swanson® Chicken Broth (Regular, Natural Goodness® *or* Certified Organic)

5 large potatoes, cut into 1-inch pieces (about 7½ cups)

½ cup light cream

2 tablespoons butter

Generous dash ground black pepper

1 can (14½ ounces) Campbell's® Turkey Gravy

PREP
15 MINUTES

COOK
20 MINUTES

1 Heat the broth and potatoes in a 3-quart saucepan over medium-high heat to a boil.

2 Reduce the heat to medium. Cover and cook for 10 minutes or until the potatoes are tender. Drain, reserving the broth.

3 Mash the potatoes with ¼ **cup** broth, cream, butter and black pepper. Add additional broth, if needed, until desired consistency. Serve with the gravy.

Ultimate Mashed Potatoes:
Stir ½ **cup** sour cream, **3** slices bacon, cooked and crumbled (reserve some for garnish), **and** ¼ **cup** chopped fresh chives into the hot mashed potatoes. Sprinkle with the reserved bacon.

Nothing completes a meal quite like

a special sweet. Make tonight a little

extra-special with these desserts.

desserts

Peach & Berry Cobbler

MAKES 6 SERVINGS

PREP
5 MINUTES

COOK
4 HOURS

Vegetable cooking spray

1 **package (16 ounces) frozen peach slices**

1 **package (16 ounces) frozen mixed berries (strawberries, blueberries *and* raspberries)**

1 **cup V8 V-Fusion® Peach Mango Juice**

1 **tablespoon cornstarch**

1 **teaspoon almond extract**

1 **package (18.25 ounces) yellow cake mix**

1 **stick butter (4 ounces), cut into pieces**

Confectioners' sugar

1 Spray the inside of a 6-quart slow cooker with the cooking spray. Place the peaches and berries into the cooker.

2 Stir the juice, cornstarch and almond extract in a small bowl. Pour into the cooker.

3 Sprinkle the cake mix over the fruit mixture. Dot with the butter.

4 Layer **8** pieces of paper towel across the top of the cooker. Place the cooker cover on top*.

5 Cook on LOW for 4 to 5 hours** or until the fruit mixture boils and thickens and the topping is cooked through. Sprinkle with the confectioners' sugar.

*The paper towels will absorb any moisture that rises to the top of the cooker.

**Do not lift the cover on the cooker at all during the first 3 hours of the cook time.

Amazing Red Devil's Food Cake

MAKES 12 SERVINGS

PREP
15 MINUTES

BAKE
35 MINUTES

COOL
40 MINUTES

2½ **cups all-purpose flour**

½ **cup unsweetened cocoa powder**

1½ **teaspoons baking soda**

¼ **teaspoon salt**

½ **cup (1 stick) butter, softened**

1¾ **cups sugar**

2 **eggs**

1 **teaspoon vanilla extract**

1½ **cups Campbell's® Tomato Juice**

Creamy Butter Frosting

1 Heat the oven to 350°F. Grease and flour **2** (8-inch) round cake pans.

2 Stir the flour, cocoa, baking soda and salt in a medium bowl.

3 Beat the butter and sugar in a large bowl with an electric mixer on medium speed until the mixture is light and fluffy. Beat in the eggs, one at a time, beating well after each addition. Beat in the vanilla extract.

4 Reduce the speed to low. Add the flour mixture alternately with the tomato juice, beating well after each addition. Pour the batter into the cake pans.

5 Bake for 35 minutes or until a toothpick inserted in the center comes out clean. Cool the cakes in the pans on wire racks for 10 minutes. Remove the cakes from the pans and cool completely on the wire racks. Frost and fill with the *Creamy Butter Frosting*. Refrigerate until ready to serve.

Creamy Butter Frosting: Place ¾ **cup** (1½ sticks) butter, softened, **1 package** (16 ounces) confectioners' sugar, ¼ **cup** milk, ½ **teaspoon** vanilla extract and ¼ **teaspoon** salt in a medium bowl. Beat with an electric mixer on low speed until the mixture is smooth. Increase the speed to medium, adding more milk, if needed, until desired consistency. Makes 2½ cups.

Chocolate Mousse Napoleons with Strawberries & Cream

MAKES 12 SERVINGS

THAW
40 MINUTES

PREP
25 MINUTES

BAKE
15 MINUTES

COOL
10 MINUTES

½ **of a 17.3-ounce package Pepperidge Farm® Puff Pastry Sheets (1 sheet)**

1 **cup heavy cream**

¼ **teaspoon ground cinnamon**

1 **cup semi-sweet chocolate pieces, melted**

2 **cups sweetened whipped cream*** *or* **whipped topping**

1½ **cups sliced strawberries**

1 **square (1 ounce) semi-sweet chocolate, melted (optional)**

Confectioners' sugar

For **2 cups sweetened whipped cream, beat **1 cup** heavy cream, **2 tablespoons** sugar and ¼ **teaspoon** vanilla extract in a chilled medium bowl with an electric mixer on high speed until stiff peaks form.*

1 Thaw the pastry sheet at room temperature for 40 minutes or until it's easy to handle. Heat the oven to 400°F.

2 Unfold the pastry sheet on a lightly floured surface. Cut the pastry sheet into **3** strips along the fold marks. Cut **each** strip into **6** rectangles, making **18** pastry rectangles. Place the pastry rectangles 1 inch apart on a baking sheet.

3 Bake for 15 minutes or until the pastries are golden. Remove the pastries from the baking sheet and cool on a wire rack. Split **each** pastry into **2** layers, making **36** layers.

4 Beat the cream and cinnamon in a large bowl with an electric mixer on high speed until stiff peaks form. Fold in the melted chocolate pieces.

5 Spread **12** pastry layers with the chocolate cream and top with **12** pastry layers. Top with the whipped cream, strawberries and remaining pastry layers. Serve immediately or cover and refrigerate for up to 4 hours.

6 Drizzle the napoleons with the melted chocolate, if desired, and sprinkle with the confectioners' sugar just before serving.

Chocolate-Cinnamon Bread Pudding

MAKES 6 SERVINGS

PREP
15 MINUTES

BAKE
40 MINUTES

12 slices Pepperidge Farm® Cinnamon Swirl Bread, any variety, cut into cubes (about 6 cups)

½ cup semi-sweet chocolate pieces

2½ cups milk

4 eggs

½ cup packed brown sugar

1 teaspoon vanilla extract

Sweetened whipped cream (optional)

1 Heat the oven to 350°F.

2 Place the bread cubes into a lightly greased 2-quart shallow baking dish. Sprinkle the chocolate pieces over the bread cubes. Beat the milk, eggs, brown sugar and vanilla extract in a small bowl with a fork or whisk. Pour the milk mixture over the bread cubes. Stir and press the bread cubes into the milk mixture to coat.

3 Bake for 40 minutes or until a knife inserted in the center comes out clean. Serve with the whipped cream, if desired.

This bread pudding can be served with the whipped cream as a dessert, or with a sprinkle of confectioners' sugar as a decadent brunch dish.

Lemon Cheesecake Mini Tartlets

MAKES 36 TARTLETS

THAW
40 MINUTES

PREP
20 MINUTES

BAKE
10 MINUTES

COOL
20 MINUTES

CHILL
10 MINUTES

½ **of a 17.3-ounce package Pepperidge Farm® Puff Pastry Sheets (1 sheet), thawed**

1 **egg, beaten**

½ **of an 8-ounce package cream cheese, softened**

½ **cup prepared lemon curd**

½ **cup thawed frozen whipped topping**

Fresh raspberries *or* blueberries

1 Heat the oven to 375°F. Lightly grease **36** (1½-inch) mini muffin-pan cups.

2 Unfold the pastry sheet on a lightly floured surface. Roll the pastry sheet into a 12-inch square. Cut into **36** (2-inch) squares. Press the pastry squares into the muffin-pan cups. Brush the top edges of the pastry squares with the egg. Prick the centers of the pastries with a fork.

3 Bake for 10 minutes or until the pastries are golden brown. Using the back of a spoon, press down the centers of the hot pastries to make an indentation. Let the pastries cool in the pans on wire racks for 10 minutes. Remove the pastry cups from the pans and let cool completely on wire racks.

To make ahead, prepare as directed above. Cover and refrigerate for up to 24 hours.

4 Beat the cream cheese in a medium bowl with an electric mixer on medium speed until smooth. Beat in the lemon curd. Fold in the whipped topping.

5 Pipe or spoon **about 1 teaspoon** cheese mixture into **each** pastry cup. Refrigerate for 10 minutes or until the set. Top **each** tartlet with **1** raspberry.

Raspberry Tiramisu Trifle

MAKES 6 SERVINGS

PREP
20 MINUTES

CHILL
1 HOUR

1 **package (8 ounces) cream cheese, softened**

1 **cup confectioners' sugar**

¼ **teaspoon ground cinnamon**

1 **cup heavy cream, whipped**

1 **package (6 ounces) Pepperidge Farm® Milano® Cookies**

⅓ **cup brewed black coffee**

1 **cup sweetened frozen raspberries, thawed and drained**

¼ **cup grated semi-sweet chocolate**

tip

Heavy cream will whip faster when the bowl and beaters are cold. Place the bowl and beaters in the freezer for about 15 minutes before using, then use the cream right from the refrigerator.

1 Beat the cream cheese in a medium bowl with an electric mixer on medium speed until smooth. Beat in the sugar and cinnamon. Fold in the whipped cream.

2 Spoon **1 cup** cheese mixture into a 4-cup trifle bowl. Dip **6** of the cookies, one at a time, into the coffee and place over the cheese layer, overlapping slightly. Spoon **2 tablespoons** raspberries over the cookies. Repeat the layers. Spread the remaining cheese mixture over the top. Garnish with the remaining cookies and raspberries. Refrigerate for 1 hour.

3 Garnish with the chocolate before serving.

Tomato Soup Spice Cupcakes

MAKES 24 SERVINGS

PREP
10 MINUTES

BAKE
20 MINUTES

COOL
20 MINUTES

After frosting, you can sprinkle the cupcakes with toasted chopped pecans or walnuts.

1 **box (about 18 ounces) spice cake mix**

1 **can (10¾ ounces) Campbell's® Condensed Tomato Soup (Regular *or* Healthy Request®)**

½ **cup water**

2 **eggs**

Store-bought *or* homemade cream cheese frosting

1 Heat the oven to 350°F. Place liners into **24** (2½-inch) muffin-pan cups.

2 Combine the cake mix, soup, water and eggs in a large bowl and mix according to the package directions. Spoon the batter into the muffin-pan cups.

3 Bake for 20 minutes or until a toothpick inserted in the center of a cupcake comes out clean.

4 Let the cupcakes cool in the pans on wire racks for 10 minutes. Remove the cupcakes from the pans and let cool completely.

5 Frost with your favorite cream cheese frosting.

Quick and Easy Chocolate Fondue

MAKES 12 SERVINGS

PREP
5 MINUTES

COOK
5 MINUTES

2 cups semi-sweet chocolate pieces

½ cup (1 stick) butter

Suggested Dippers: **Pepperidge Farm® Cinnamon Swirl Bread, toasted and cut into strips; Pepperidge Farm® Chessmen® Cookies; Pepperidge Farm® Gingerman Homestyle Cookies; Pepperidge Farm® Milano® Cookies**

1 Cook and stir the chocolate and butter in an 8-inch heavy skillet over low heat for 5 minutes or until the chocolate is melted and smooth.

2 Pour the chocolate mixture into a fondue pot or a decorative bowl. Serve warm with the *Dippers.*

*You can also use this chocolate mixture to make festive chocolate and candy-coated puff pastry strips: Thaw **1** sheet Pepperidge Farm® Puff Pastry. Unfold the pastry sheet on a lightly floured surface and roll into a 12-inch square. Cut into **72** (4×½-inch) strips and place onto baking sheets. Bake at 400° F. for 20 minutes or until golden brown. Dip the pastry strips in the warm chocolate mixture and sprinkle with crushed candy canes. Place on wax paper-lined baking sheets. Refrigerate or let stand at room temperature until chocolate is set.*

Almond Orange Pithivier

MAKES 12 SERVINGS

THAW	1 **cup sliced blanched almonds**
40 MINUTES	⅓ **cup granulated sugar**
BAKE	¼ **cup (½ stick) unsalted butter, softened**
25 MINUTES	2 **eggs**
COOL	1 **tablespoon grated orange zest**
20 MINUTES	1 **teaspoon vanilla extract**

1 **cup sliced blanched almonds**

⅓ **cup granulated sugar**

¼ **cup (½ stick) unsalted butter, softened**

2 **eggs**

1 **tablespoon grated orange zest**

1 **teaspoon vanilla extract**

1 **package (17.3 ounces) Pepperidge Farm® Puff Pastry Sheets, thawed**

1 **teaspoon water**

Confectioners' sugar

1 Heat the oven to 375°F. Place the almonds, sugar, butter, **1** egg, orange zest and vanilla extract into a food processor. Cover and process until the mixture is smooth.

2 Unfold **1** pastry sheet on a lightly floured surface. Roll the pastry sheet into an 11-inch square. Cut into a 10-inch circle. Repeat with the remaining pastry sheet.

3 Place **1** pastry circle onto a baking sheet. Spread the almond mixture on the pastry circle to within 1 inch of the edge. Beat the remaining egg and the water in a small bowl with a fork or whisk. Brush the edge of the pastry circle with the egg mixture. Place the remaining pastry circle over the filling. Crimp the edges of the circles together with a fork.

4 Bake for 25 minutes or until the pastry is golden brown. Remove the pastry from the baking sheet and let cool completely on a wire rack. Sprinkle the pastry with the confectioners' sugar.

Berry Bordeaux Desserts

MAKES 12 SERVINGS

24 **Pepperidge Farm® Bordeaux® Cookies**

1 **cup heavy cream**

¼ **cup sugar**

1 **teaspoon vanilla extract**

3 **cups mixed berries***

Mint leaves (optional)

*Use a combination of sliced strawberries, raspberries, blackberries **and** blueberries.*

PREP
20 MINUTES

CHILL
3 HOURS

1 Place **12** cookies into a 2-quart shallow baking dish.

2 Beat the heavy cream, **2 tablespoons** sugar and vanilla extract in a medium bowl with an electric mixer on high speed until stiff peaks form.

3 Spoon the whipped cream in the baking dish. Top with the remaining cookies. Cover and refrigerate for 3 hours or until the cookies are soft.

4 Stir the berries with the remaining sugar in a medium bowl. Spoon the berry mixture over the cookie mixture. Garnish with the mint, if desired.

VOLUME MEASUREMENTS (dry)

1/8 teaspoon = 0.5 mL
1/4 teaspoon = 1 mL
1/2 teaspoon = 2 mL
3/4 teaspoon = 4 mL
1 teaspoon = 5 mL
1 tablespoon = 15 mL
2 tablespoons = 30 mL
1/4 cup = 60 mL
1/3 cup = 75 mL
1/2 cup = 125 mL
2/3 cup = 150 mL
3/4 cup = 175 mL
1 cup = 250 mL
2 cups = 1 pint = 500 mL
3 cups = 750 mL
4 cups = 1 quart = 1 L

VOLUME MEASUREMENTS (fluid)

1 fluid ounce (2 tablespoons) = 30 mL
4 fluid ounces (1/2 cup) = 125 mL
8 fluid ounces (1 cup) = 250 mL
12 fluid ounces (1 1/2 cups) = 375 mL
16 fluid ounces (2 cups) = 500 mL

WEIGHTS (mass)

1/2 ounce = 15 g
1 ounce = 30 g
3 ounces = 90 g
4 ounces = 120 g
8 ounces = 225 g
10 ounces = 285 g
12 ounces = 360 g
16 ounces = 1 pound = 450 g

DIMENSIONS

1/16 inch = 2 mm
1/8 inch = 3 mm
1/4 inch = 6 mm
1/2 inch = 1.5 cm
3/4 inch = 2 cm
1 inch = 2.5 cm

OVEN TEMPERATURES

250°F = 120°C
275°F = 140°C
300°F = 150°C
325°F = 160°C
350°F = 180°C
375°F = 190°C
400°F = 200°C
425°F = 220°C
450°F = 230°C

BAKING PAN AND DISH EQUIVALENTS

Utensil	Size in Inches	Size in Centimeters	Volume	Metric Volume
Baking or Cake Pan (square or rectangular)	8×8×2	20×20×5	8 cups	2 L
	9×9×2	23×23×5	10 cups	2.5 L
	13×9×2	33×23×5	12 cups	3 L
Loaf Pan	8½×4½×2½	21×11×6	6 cups	1.5 L
	9×9×3	23×13×7	8 cups	2 L
Round Layer Cake Pan	8×1½	20×4	4 cups	1 L
	9×1½	23×4	5 cups	1.25 L
Pie Plate	8×1½	20×4	4 cups	1 L
	9×1½	23×4	5 cups	1.25 L
Baking Dish or Casserole			1 quart/4 cups	1 L
			1½ quart/6 cups	1.5 L
			2 quart/8 cups	2 L
			3 quart/12 cups	3 L